The Decline of the
Age of Oil

The Decline of the Age of Oil

Brian J. Fleay
B Eng, M Eng Sc, MIE Aust, MAWWA

Pluto Press Australia

To Emma, Ted, Arnold and Peter for reviewing the
many drafts of this book. To my wife, Lesley, for
forbearance and for preparation of the figures.

First published in December 1995 by
Pluto Press Australia Limited
Locked Bag 199, Annandale, NSW 2038

Cover design by Trevor Hood

Index by Neale Towart

Printed and bound by Southwood Press, 80 Chapel Street,
Marrickville, NSW 2204

Australian Cataloguing in Publication Data

Fleay, B.J (Brian J.)
  The decline of the age of oil
  Petrol politics: Australia's road ahead

  Bibliography.
  Includes index.
  ISBN 1 86403 021 6.

  1. Petroleum industry and trade — Australia. 2. Petroleum products — Australia.
  3. Energy development — Australia. 4. Energy policy — Australia. I. Title

333.790994

Table of Contents

List of Figures

List of Tables

Abbreviations & Glossary

ABARE	Australian Bureau of Agricultural and Resource Economics
AGA	Australian Gas Association
AMEC	Australian Mineral and Energy Council
APEA	Australian Petroleum Exploration Association
barrel	One barrel of oil equals 159.987 litres. One million barrels equals 0.159987 gigalitres (GL)
BP	British Petroleum
BRS	Bureau of Resource Sciences
BTCE	Bureau of Transport and Communications Economics
CIS	Commonwealth of Independent States
CNG	Compressed Natural Gas
EPR	Energy Profit Ratio
EROI	Energy Return On Investment
FSU	Former Soviet Union
GDP	Gross Domestic Product (the gross national product (GNP) minus the net payments on foreign investments)
giga	Prefix for 1 billion (1000 million)
GJ	gigajoule (equivalent to 277.78 kWh)
GJ/$GDP	gigajoules per dollar Gross Domestic Product

GNP	Gross National Product (the total monetary value of all the goods and services produced in a nation during a certain period of time)
Joule	A unit measuring energy
kcal	kilocalorie (1000 calories, a unit of energy)
kWh	kilowatt hour (a unit measuring energy)
LPG	Liquefied petroleum gas
mega	Prefix for 1 million
million	1000 thousand
m.bls/d	Million barrels per day
MJ	megajoule
NOCs	National Oil Companies (government owned)
OECD	Organization of Economic Cooperation and Development
OPEC	Organization of Petroleum Exporting Countries
PJ	petajoule (1000 million million joules)
R/P	Reserves/Production ratio (ratio of proven oil reserves to current production rate)
trillion	Thousand billion
VLCC	Very large crude carrier

Foreword

This book is a modern day prophecy. It suggests we are facing a future that is full of potential disaster due to the depletion of the world economy's most precious resource, oil. But like all prophecy from former times it sketches out how we can avoid the collapse of our cities and transport systems if we act decisively.

Prophecy of this kind has always been subject to derision. There are always those who say 'all is well when all is not well' as Ezekiel commented in 590 BC. And there are always those who brush aside resource crises:

'The bricks are fallen but we will build in hewnstone,
The sycamores are hacked down but we will use cedars instead',

so Isaiah wryly commented in the 8th century BC about a city that indeed collapsed.

Similar prophecy to this book was made in the 1970s when the first two oil crises struck. But since the might of the West crushed Iraq in the third oil crisis the world has felt as though oil depletion was off the agenda. Middle Eastern suppliers are now in crisis financially because they can't make enough money from such low-priced oil. Surely we can't be facing a global oil depletion crisis?

Brian Fleay's analysis goes beyond the short term markets to the underlying geophysical principles. His evidence is gathered from many sources all pointing in one direction: the 'golden century of oil', as Campbell calls it, is about to move inexorably from growth to decline.

Much can be done in response, but the first task is to read this book and think about it.

Associate Professor Peter Newman
Director, Institute of Science and Technology Policy
Murdoch University
Western University

1
Energy and Economics

If we have available energy, we may maintain life and produce every material requisite necessary. That is why the flow of energy should be the primary concern of economics. (Soddy 1926)

Oil production in the major producing regions of the world is reaching its peak and beginning a decline. A fifty-year transition period began in the USA in 1970. The former Soviet Union's (FSU's) oil production peaked in 1989 and has suffered rapid decline since. The remainder of the producing regions outside the Arabian Gulf are expected to peak by the year 2005. The Arabian Gulf region, with two thirds of world oil reserves, is likely to peak last in about 2020. Production of oil in the world as a whole is likely to peak some ten years earlier.

The remaining unexplored regions are limited and mostly in remote and expensive to develop regions, like the Arctic Ocean or offshore in deep water on the continental slopes. This oil will not be cheap.

The world's transport systems run largely on oil, as does much of mechanised agriculture. Oil, being a liquid, is easy to store, transport and dispense accurately, thus is the most economically efficient of the fossil fuels.

The production life cycle of petroleum fuels when graphed has a bell-shaped curve: the peak production rate occurs when about half of the economically extractable oil has been produced. The first half of oil production rising to the peak is the cheapest and most economically effective, as will be explained later. The reverse is the case for the second half, with the onset of declining production. The fossil fuels are becoming a constraint to economic activity much sooner than most people think, which is why the world as we know it is undergoing more and more rapid structural change.

Energy and economics are intimately related, but contemporary economics is seriously flawed in the way it incorporates energy into its framework. We need to explore some of the linkages between energy and economics in order to understand the fascinating story of oil, where we have come from and where we now need to go. For it is certain that our economic future will be quite unlike our experiences in the twentieth century.

An energy theory of value

Two ecologists, Howard T. Odum and Robert Costanza, have been in the forefront of those attempting to forge an alternative economic approach to contemporary neoclassical theory. Their viewpoint is based on an energy theory of value (Odum 1971; Odum & Odum 1981; Costanza 1981). The new approach sees all value as ultimately derived from nature, unlike neoclassical theory where value is founded primarily in human relationships through exchanges in the marketplace. The new theory does not displace contemporary economics, rather it integrates it within its proper environmental context.

From an energy perspective all economic activity is ultimately driven by energy flows from nature, as shown in Figure 1.1. This emerging model says the human economy is a *thermodynamically open system embedded in the environment* and depends on a net inflow of energy, natural resources, and other services from the environment. Value ultimately has its source in natural resources in direct proportion to the degree of concentration (order) or complex structure stored in those resources and in inverse proportion to the physical energy cost of finding and extracting that order. For example, a high-grade mineral requires less energy to extract from nature than does a low-grade mineral. Production and distribution of goods and services is powered from outside the economic system by a one way flow of high-grade energy which is irreversibly dissipated. In this line of reasoning energy is the organising principle from which all values — economic, social, environmental, aesthetic and political — are ultimately derived.

The stock of natural resources on which the economic system operates is produced initially by natural biological, geological, physical and chemical processes powered by solar energy and the internal heat of the earth. These processes have given rise to a rich, varied and diverse range of complex natural forms and organisms, a living planet. Natural energies from the past have upgraded and concentrated these elements to become resources that can be used in the human economy

Figure 1.1

ORGANIC/THERMODYNAMIC ECONOMIC MODEL

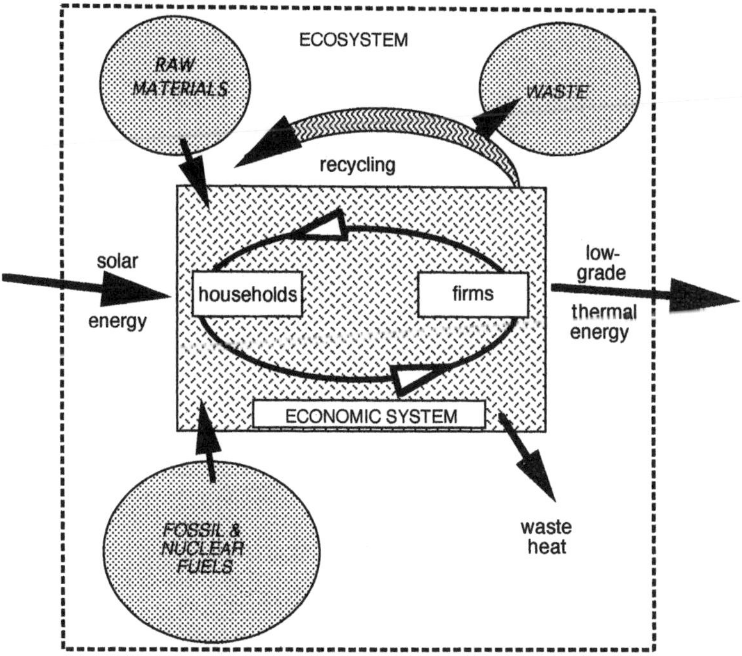

The economic system is an open one exchanging energy/matter with the ecosystem. The economic system dissipates energy irreversibly and degrades matter for recycling through the ecosystem.

to produce useful goods and services, for example minerals, coal, oil, nutrients for plants, living organisms, the atmosphere, water. Useful energy and matter must be extracted from nature for the process to continue.

All matter and energy used in the economy are ultimately discharged as waste to the environment. The matter can be recycled naturally through the environment to become natural resources again. The time required can vary from weeks for some organic wastes to millions of years for most minerals. All such recycling operations consume or dissipate energy into a low-grade or unavailable form. Once water in rivers has reached the ocean it can no longer shape the landscape by erosion, its energy has dissipated as heat. Energy, however, cannot be recycled. You can only ever burn a piece of coal once. Not all the energy in nature is available to do useful work. Some must be mobilised to make nature's energy stock available in forms that living systems can use. The fraction left in a useful or available form is called free energy. Such available free energy is the ultimate limiting resource for all forms of life.

From a human perspective all economic costs are ultimately an energy cost. In this context human labour can also be considered as an active high-quality energy source with high information processing, communication, organising and control capabilities. Gaining knowledge and information, preserving it and passing it on to future generations is generally an energy-intensive activity.

This economic model says the human economy is like a living organism. Its metabolic processes require a continual one way flow of complex organised energy and matter from nature to replenish and maintain the economic structures inherited from the past, to build new ones and to produce the goods and services that humans need. Degraded energy and matter are returned to the environment. Like any living organism a particular economy has a life history linked with its environment, has growing and declining phases and makes way for its successors. The fact that pollution control and environmental care are becoming standard economic considerations confirms this.

Odum and Costanza maintain that a significant factor driving natural selection, both in nature and human affairs, is access to free energy together with the efficiency and differential rates of its use among competitors. They say *maximum power* (the trade-off between high energy efficiency achieved at a slow rate and lower energy efficiencies achieved at faster rates) is an important criterion by which ecological or economic systems select surviving behaviour patterns. A simple example is the competition for long-haul passengers between rail, subsonic jet aircraft and the supersonic Concorde. Rail travel has three times the energy efficiency of subsonic jets, but achieves this at a slow speed; that is by a slow rate of energy use, a low power output. Concorde is only one third as energy efficient as large subsonic jets, there is a rapid rate of energy use largely wasted in pushing the aircraft through the air. Concorde does not produce worthwhile time savings for passengers compared with subsonic aircraft as it does not affect the significant time required to travel to and from airports. Concorde has never been a commercial success and subsonic jets have captured most long-haul passenger air traffic. Those business people travelling by subsonic jet are able to capture other sources of free energy ahead of the slower but more energy-efficient train travellers, who lose out. The early bird gets the worm.

The real world, of course, is far more complex than this simple example. There are always many such processes interweaving in complex ways. As abundant high-quality petroleum fuels become scarce and more expensive the situation will change, perhaps favouring rail again. Energy efficiency may become more important and rail can use alternative fuels to petroleum far more readily than aircraft. Scarce petroleum may need to be diverted from transport to agriculture. We must eat before we can travel.

Odum says the *maximum power principle* lies at the heart of many human behaviours, being the principal mechanism in natural and cultural selection, and in economic development. He says moral, ethical and all psychological phenomena are derived from incorporating such surviving behaviour patterns as ultimate values. Traditional religious values evolved to regulate the use and abuse of power, based on the energy sources available to humans at the time. Today we have harnessed the new power sources of fossil fuels and nuclear energy but have not yet evolved the moral and ethical values and corresponding institutions needed to regulate their use in human affairs in an ecologically sustainable way. Creating these values and institutions is a central and urgent task of our time.

This does not justify all-out competition, Herbert Spencer's nature bloody in tooth and claw. Systems which follow that path exclusively quickly dissipate energy and exhaust resources, are in danger of cancerous unregulated growth. The majority of living systems survive longer by developing complex arrays of mutually supportive relationships that maximise system power and reinforce adaptive survival patterns. Competition has a subordinate role within the larger supportive system.

That is how the New Zealand team won the 1995 America's Cup yacht race. The crew were chosen first and then worked cooperatively with the designers and builders to construct a yacht that integrated with them. A powerful synergy between crew and boat developed that maximised the power obtained from the wind; winning 41 out of 42 races. There was an interweaving of challenge, teamwork and competition (*West Australian* 1995). The other teams did not have this behaviour pattern

Business management practices are also evolving in this direction, consciously drawing upon emerging organic and ecologically based concepts, rejecting older mechanistic management philosophies. A US management consultant, Harrison Owen, says management theory has commonly been a discussion about control from the top and now largely irrelevant. He says there was a misconception that organisations are closed systems *with impermeable boundaries, therefore predictable* and capable of central coordination and direction. Those were the days when bosses were bosses (*Business Review Weekly* 1994).

Owen describes this view as a fabrication of the scientific imagination. Laboratory conditions have always been artificially closed with impermeable boundaries to limit disturbances to experiments and to isolate causes. The world of management cannot be isolated in this way. In the real world, we put up a pretence, we cannot afford to admit that organisations are arbitrary creations with open boundaries, *hence not totally predictable*, and therefore are participative systems where nobody can be totally in control, which means we all are. Conflicts between the aims of the individual and organisations are becoming an expensive luxury. However, by operating towards others as if boundaries are open, that is minimal or non existent, helps to create many dynamic opportunities for interchange and productivity that are hard to beat. The generation of innovation requires stimulation, openness and interchange, things that best occur with unguarded boundaries (*Business Review Weekly* 1994). Organisations have no choice but to evolve in a participative cooperative direction or die.

Mental activities are becoming the centre of wealth creation rather than just a factor of production, according to Dr Michael Gordy, moderator of the Myer Foundation's Craniana Symposium, 'Knowledge in the 21st Century'. The outcome is a dramatic change in the nature of ownership. Intellect and ideas are not tangible and portable in the way property is. When an object is sold the seller no longer has it; when knowledge is sold the seller still possesses it. Wealth becomes reflected more by what a person is able to share than in possessions. One consequence is that neoclassical economic theory's emphasis on contractual relationships and individual property rights is becoming less relevant. In a knowledge economy competition for assets is not the fundamental impetus in wealth creation. Knowledge is developed through sharing, not competition. People develop understanding together, they cannot do it individually (*Business Review Weekly* 1994a).

Costanza has extended Odum's original analysis offering empirical evidence that supports one necessary condition for an energy theory of value in economics: the relative prices of goods can be explained by their relative embodied energy cost. Fossil fuel energy embodied in goods and services correlates closely with market determined dollar values when the analysis is comprehensive enough (Costanza 1980, 1981).

The energy theory of value is described more fully in Hall, Cleveland and Kaufmann's *Energy and Resource Quality* (1986, pp. 1–150).This theory's advocates do not see their views as being a substitute for other theories nor as having all the answers, but rather as a necessary complement to them. Their approach is essential for mid- to long-term economic assessments when changes in resource quality can significantly affect outcomes, development patterns and social structure. Fossil fuels have built the contemporary industrialised world and are a key factor in understanding its future.

Energy profit ratio

Another key concept in the energy theory of value is Energy Profit Ratio (EPR), sometimes known as Energy Return On Investment (EROI). EPR is defined as:

$$EPR = \frac{\text{Energy content of fuel}}{\text{Energy used in its production}}$$

The energy is measured in joules. The denominator is the sum of all direct and indirect energy inputs embodied in the materials, goods and services used to produce the fuel, including information and people. For industrial fuels these energy inputs include sources such as coal, oil, natural gas, hydro and nuclear electricity. Direct solar energy is not always included in the calculation unless for a specific purpose even though such energy always makes a contribution that is often substantial for the activity under study, for example agriculture. The larger the value of EPR the higher the energy quality and the more economically useful is the fuel. As the energy needed to produce these high-quality fuels is low so the industry needed to produce them is small relative to the wider economy it serves. Consequently, free available energy to do useful work in the economy is large as the energy industry does not consume much energy, and is for that reason relatively small. It is in this sense that the phrase 'high-energy quality' is used in this book.

Another way of looking at energy quality in the economy is to evaluate free energy. Only free energy is available to perform useful services.

Free energy = Energy content of fuel − Energy used in the fuel's production

Importance of fuel type

Both the EPR and the free energy approaches have limitations, as they do not distinguish between the relative usefulness of different forms of energy such as heat, electricity, coal, oil or natural gas. Yet fuel type is as important as free energy and EPR.

Coal-fired power stations waste two thirds of the energy potential of the coal as waste heat in the smokestack and in the water used to condense steam from the turbines. The flexibility, versatility and precision with which electricity can be applied on all scales, its information and control capabilities, make it a more economically productive form of energy, despite 70 per cent of the heat from burning coal being lost to the environment during its production.

In the USA fossil fuels used in power stations produce 2.6 to 14.3 times the dollar value in the economy when transformed into electricity than when used directly as a fuel (Gever, Kaufmann, Skole & Vörösmarty 1991, p. 269). For fossil fuels nature did this energy quality upgrading from primary biomass over millions of years.

Petroleum is a more effective fuel than coal for most purposes. A coal-fired locomotive uses five times the thermal energy that a diesel locomotive uses to pull the same train.

Oil and gas in the USA generate more dollar value per joule than coal by factors ranging from 1.3 to 2.45 (Hall et al. 1986, p. 55). The fluid petroleum fuels are easier and cheaper to store, transport and use with precision and flexibility, and petroleum is easier to use on both small and large scales compared with coal. (Try running a Victa lawnmower on coal.) Oil will produce more dollar value per joule than coal where both have the same EPR.

Hence oil products drive almost all the world's powered transport systems. Furthermore, products produced using coal and electricity require significant transport for their production, distribution to markets and for the disposal of wastes. The industries and services using coal and electricity require petroleum-powered transport to be economically effective and viable.

This has significant structural implications for the economy as high-quality oil production peaks over the next two decades and dominates all strategic considerations.

Energy, welfare and economics (GDP)

Energy used in the energy industry does not directly contribute to human welfare. By welfare are meant the benefits and useful service arising from economic activity. Energy is the means to an end, not the end itself. Where the EPR is low, use of that energy source may diminish welfare, especially for countries heavily dependent on poor-quality fossil fuels.

Gross Domestic Product (GDP) is an index used by economists to measure in dollars the traded economic output of a country or region. The energy extraction industry's contribution to GDP should be subtracted from the gross GDP figure to get a truer measure of the welfare component of GDP. Only free or net energy contributes to welfare. Hitherto this discrepancy has been of minor significance, but this will not be the case in the future as high-quality petroleum fuels are depleted and the energy industry starts consuming proportionately more energy than in the past. GDP, of course, says nothing about equity or access to wealth.

As its EPR approaches one, production of a fuel becomes progressively uneconomic, relative free energy diminishes, and the energy industry becomes a bigger component of the economy. Only for exceptional and limited purposes could a community afford to produce a fuel with an EPR of less than one.

Improvements in the energy efficiency of processes used to produce fuels can increase their EPR, provided the improvements do not consume more energy than they save. An EPR can be calculated for such improvements. Technology and efficiency improvements always consume more energy than most people think.

Chapter 5 shows that EPR considerations significantly limit the economic viability and effectiveness of alternative energy sources to petroleum fuels as we have known them.

Figure 1.2

ENERGY PROFIT RATIO FOR OIL AND GAS EXTRACTION OVER THE PRODUCTION LIFE CYCLE, LOUISIANA, USA

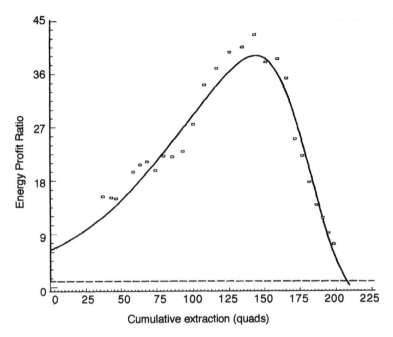

Cumulative extraction (quads)

Energy & Resource Quality: Hall, Cleveland & Kaufmann 1986, p. 186

EPR profile over the oil and gas production cycle

The EPR profile for oil and gas production in Louisiana, USA, is shown in Figure 1.2. Note that the profile rose to a peak when two thirds of the ultimate oil from this field was produced. Chapter 2 will demonstrate that the peak production rate for oil occurs when about half the ultimate production from a field has been produced.

So for Louisiana both the EPR and production peaks have occurred well before production ceases.

Similar life-cycle profiles can be expected for other oil and gas fields, though each will have its own unique features. Nevertheless, the peaking of both production and EPR in the middle range of ulti-mate production can be expected. It is too early in the coal production cycle to draw similar conclusions from an empirical base. However, the most accessible and easily mined coal deposits with high EPR are most likely being mined first.

Certainly petroleum is the cheapest and most economically effective fuel produced in the phase rising to the production peak. Post-peak the reverse is the case: the onset of an ever steeper decline in production, then of economic effectiveness of the fuel. None of the alternatives to oil are likely to match it in economic effectiveness and availability, a subject discussed in chapter 5.

Neoclassical economics

Having looked at linkages between energy and economics at a basic physical level, we now need to briefly examine contemporary neoclassical economics to understand its weaknesses where energy is concerned and to understand its place in the energy theory of value.

The traditional neoclassical model of the economic process is shown in Figure 1.3. The model says households own or control the factors of production (land, labour and capital), and that firms buy or rent from households in return for the factor payments of wages, rents and royalties. Households, of course, range from those of millionaires to those of the unemployed. Firms sell goods and services back to households in return for personal consumption expenditure. The model says the process occurs in a thermodynamically *closed system* in which the factors of production and finished goods and services cycle endlessly between firms and households (Hall et al. 1986, p. 36). Land in this context is nature, the environment. Energy is implicitly derived from land and does not have a central role in the theory. The fundamentals of neoclassical theory had their origins in eighteenth-century rationalism, before the development of the science of energy in the nineteenth century.

Neoclassical economics is the study of how to distribute among humans the effects of natural resource surpluses or shortages. It is not a process for predicting when they will occur or how large they will be, or what the consequences might be. Rather, the central aim of this economics is to be a science of human relationships in the marketplace. Classical and neoclassical economic theories say fuel and other natural resources are necessary factors of production, but believe these factors are not important enough to warrant the integration of the laws of energy and matter into economic theory.

Economics is almost silent on the impacts of resource gathering and use on the human spirit, health and ecosystems. Such impacts are regarded as *external* to the economic system and are largely ignored by the profession because they cannot be priced. Land, 'the forces of nature', becomes property in human relationships. The contribution of nature to economic activity is by implication a free gift.

Figure 1.3
NEOCLASSICAL MODEL OF ECONOMIC PRODUCTION

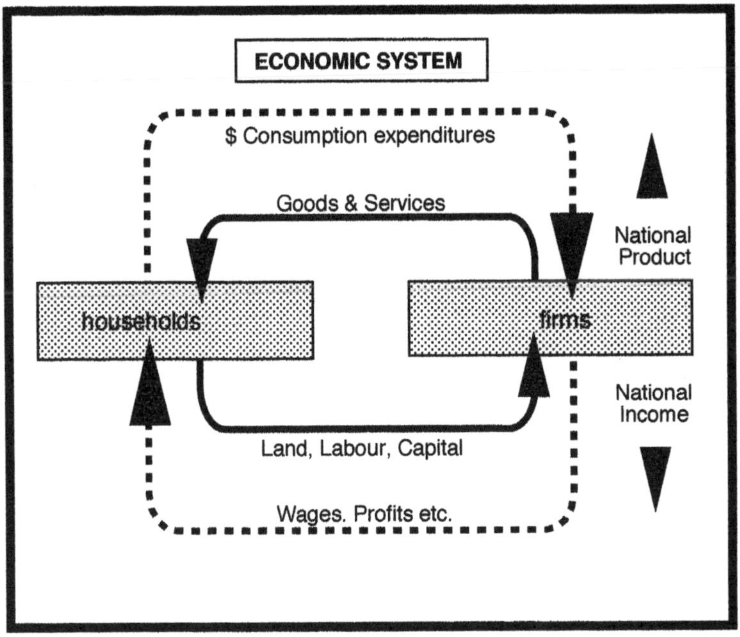

A circular flow in a closed system.
No energy or matter exchanges with the environment or ecosystem.

Neither matter nor energy enters or exits this system. Nature (land) may be finite, but it is seen as a sector of the economy for which the other sectors of capital and labour can be substituted without limiting growth. Land, labour and capital are seen as independent entities, mutually interchangeable. Resources from nature are not a constraint, and technology can always provide substitutions for those depleted (Daly & Cobb 1989, pp. 97–117). In most neoclassical analyses the economy is the total system and nature the sub-system. The reverse is the case. Hall et al. in chapters 18 to 22 examine the exchanges of matter and energy by plants and animals in nature, which could also be considered subsystems.

This circular flow model may represent dollar flows over the short term while changes in resource quality from nature are not significant. But the physical quantities that give value to those dollars cannot flow in circular fashion, nor can they replenish themselves.

Elements of the neoclassical model are embedded in the energy theory of value, but limited in their functioning by environmental constraints. Goods and services *are* exchanged in the marketplace, human relationships and perceptions *do* influence their value and price in the short term. But the ultimate source of all value comes from nature's energy flows. As Sir William Soddy says:

> The laws expressing the relations between energy and matter ... necessarily come first ... in the whole record of human experience, and they control, in the last resort, the rise and fall of political systems, the freedom and bondage of nations, the movement of commerce and industry, the origin of wealth and poverty, and the general welfare of the race. (Soddy 1926)

2
Oil Production is Going Over the Hill

Hubbert's forecasts

In the 1950s a US geologist, M. K. Hubbert, developed a method to estimate US oil and gas reserves and their future rate of exploitation. He used the mathematics of the logistic equation together with discovery and production statistics. He believed exploration would be slow and ineffective at first, due to inexperience and lack of demand; that it would quickly become rewarding; and ultimately would again become ineffective as most of the oil was found.

As would be expected, the very large oil and gas fields are usually found and brought into production first, because they are large and easy to find. These geological formations are very conspicuous when exploration begins. Sophisticated techniques are rarely needed for their discovery. They are the most prolific producers of cheap oil and have a long life.

Hubbert believed that the rate of oil discovery and then of production would initially only be constrained by the scale of exploration effort and the market for oil. The resource itself would not be limiting. However, by the second half of the production cycle, after most of the oil has been found, he showed that the discovery rate has already begun to decline. Geological constraints start to limit the rate of extraction, production peaks and also starts to decline. The relative energy cost of extracting oil starts to increase.

Hubbert used the logistic equation as it describes such relationships by combining in the one mathematical formula an exponential

Figure 2.1

IDEALISED HUBBERT CURVES FOR DISCOVERY, PRODUCTION RATES AND RESERVES

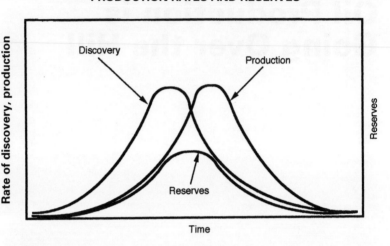

growth component and a growth-retarding factor. It is widely used in population and resource studies. Based on this view the profiles of both annual discovery and oil production rates form bell-shaped curves when graphed over time.

Peak or maximum production is reached when about half of the ultimate *economic* production has been produced — the top of the bell-shaped production curve. It goes 'over the hill'. Figure 2.1 shows idealised Hubbert curves. Note that the peak discovery rate precedes the peak production rate and that the proven reserves peak is reached between these two peaks (Hubbert 1967; 1969, pp. 158–242; Gever et al. 1991, pp. 54–74; Hall et al. 1986, pp. 176–182).

Hall, Cleveland and Kaufmann (1986, p. 187) fitted data for historical oil and gas production in Louisiana, USA to the logistic equation and obtained a very high correlation between theory and production data from 1922 to 1982.

In 1956 Hubbert accurately predicted both the year, 1973, and size of the peak in the lower forty-eight US states. This analysis was repeated by Hubbert in 1974 and again in 1981 by Gever, Kaufmann, Skole and Vörösmarty who adjusted the curve with more recent data and corrected for some inconsistencies in Hubbert's original work. These arose from the regulatory operations of the Texas Railroad Commission. The results were almost identical and are shown in Figure 2.2.

Oil production in the USA peaked over twenty years ago, ten to twelve years after the discovery rate peaked. Over 80 per cent of ultimate US oil production has already been produced.

Figure 2.2

ANNUAL RATES OF PRODUCTION IN THE LOWER 48 STATES OF THE USA

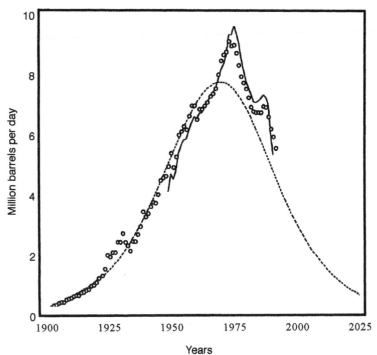

Years

Note: Rates predicted by Hubbert curve (dotted line), rates predicted by Kaufmann (1991) (solid), and actual values (open circles).

Beyond Oil: Gever, Kaufmann, and Vörösmarty, p. xxxi.

Even with the vagaries of wars, business cycles and political manipulation of prices and production, the fit between Hubbert's prediction and observation is amazingly close. His predictions allowed for efficiency improvements in oil extraction and included production from known reserves and from undiscovered fields. Government and industry experts laughed off Hubbert's projection as 'absurd' when he first announced it, but history has vindicated his position. Many knowledgeable people now accept his method as valid (Gever et al. 1991, pp. 54–74).

Hubbert's analysis and Kaufmann's modification show that domestic US oil supplies will be effectively depleted by 2020. By then the supply and quality of remaining oil will have become so low that other fuels will be used for most purposes, where and if they are available — a sobering conclusion.

Another US writer, Charles Phipps (1993), has confirmed these predictions using a different statistical approach. He came to the following conclusions:

● Major fields older than fifty years remain highly significant to current US production and reserves.

● Except for relatively unexplored prospective areas such as Alaska and California offshore, the future discovery of major US fields is statistically unlikely.

● Most presently producing major US fields will be essentially depleted (greater than 90 per cent of *present* reserves produced) within fifteen to twenty-five years.

● Without additional major field discoveries the total US oil-producing rate will decline substantially over the next decade to 2005.

Furthermore, the well-head EPR of US oil and gas production is also declining, as illustrated in Figure 2.3. Note that the energy used to transport and refine oil and gas is not included in this calculation. The trends shown in Figures 2.2 and 2.3 are cumulative. Free energy from US oil and gas is therefore declining even faster than gross production.

Figure 2.3

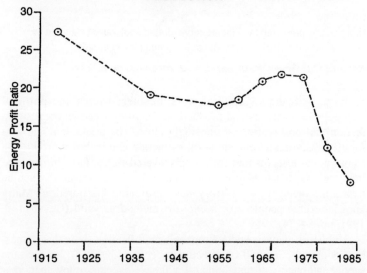

ENERGY PROFIT RATIO FOR US DOMESTIC PETROLEUM PRODUCTION

Note: Does not include transportation or refining energy.

Beyond Oil: Gever, Kaufmann, and Vörösmarty, p. 63.

Oil and gas found in the USA has fallen steadily from about forty barrels per foot drilled in 1945 to about eighteen barrels per foot drilled in 1978. The energy cost of drilling and extracting per foot drilled has been increasing over the same period. The trend shows that the energy cost of finding and extracting oil and gas will equal the energy content of that found around the year 2005. Higher oil prices will not change the situation, as costs go up with the price of oil. That is why exploration for oil and gas in the USA is winding down. Companies are, of course, moving to more prospective areas elsewhere.

US natural gas production also peaked in the 1970s. Figure 2.4 shows the Hubbert curve for natural gas, which is likely to be substantially depleted some time after 2020. Oil and gas currently comprise 70 per cent of the USA's energy budget.

Figure 2.4

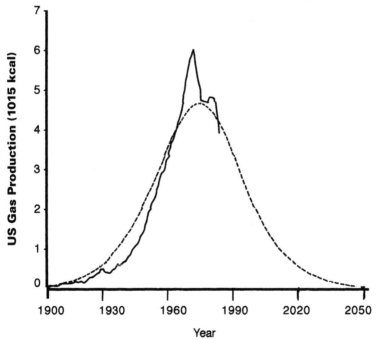

Note: Dotted line is projection, solid line is actual production

Beyond Oil: Gever, Kaufmann, and Vörösmarty, p. 59.

According to the Ottawa firm Natural Resources Canada, growing demand for gas in North America is likely to exceed declining supply from 1998 (*Oil & Gas Journal* 1995a). Most gas being developed now lies in mature areas where deliverability can be increased by development drilling in already producing fields. Spending is not needed for geophysical surveys, wildcat wells or infrastructure such as pipelines — all necessary to open up new fields. Gas prices do not allow for these extra frontier costs. A price increase is inevitable by 1998 to support such gas exploration and development.

The USA is fast approaching the depletion of its domestic economically recoverable petroleum resources — the first major province to do so. The USA now imports 50 per cent of its oil, expected to be over 55 per cent by 2000 and approaching 65 per cent by 2005. Twenty-five per cent of global oil production is consumed by the USA. Furthermore, the USA is the world's most intensely explored petroleum province. In 1975 there was one exploratory or production well for every 1.6 square kilometres of sedimentary rock. Since giant oil fields stretch for many kilometres the likelihood of new bonanzas is remote (Gever et al. 1991, pp. 54–74).

A great public outcry followed an oil spill from drilling operations offshore from Los Angeles in the early 1970s, leading to bans on petroleum exploration off the US east and west coasts. The *Exxon Valdez* tanker oil spill off Alaska in 1991 reinforced public opposition to offshore oil operations. Yet these areas may contain up to 30 billion barrels of economic oil resources, according to the US Interior Department. However, this only equals five years of US consumption, about the size of proven reserves, and the timing of US oil depletion would only be marginally extended if the drilling restrictions were lifted. Up to ten years of effort would be required before significant production was possible. Important gas resources may be present as well (*Oil & Gas Journal* 1994a). Election of a Republican Party dominated US Congress in 1994 has increased the chances that offshore drilling restrictions will be relaxed.

The USA has abundant coal resources compared with petroleum. It is too early in the coal production cycle to apply Hubbert's method as the statistical base is inadequate. However, coal has been mined in the north-eastern USA since the early eighteenth century. Thinner and steeper coal seams are now being mined, and open-cut coalmining, with its high energy cost for removing and replacing overburden, has expanded in the western USA. These developments are reflected in the declining EPR for coal since the late 1960s. The quality of coal being mined is declining and the longer term implications are not yet clear (Hall et al. 1986, p. 56).

Production of fossil fuels ceases to be economic when the energy expended in finding and producing the fuel approaches the energy content of the fuel produced, as illustrated in Figure 1.2.

One consequence of these bell-shaped profiles for production and EPR is that oil and natural gas become progressively more expensive in the declining production phase and therefore of declining economic effectiveness. In the phase rising to the peak the reverse was the case (Gever et al. 1991, pp. 54–74; Hall et al. 1986, pp. 176–82). This fact is of major significance for the future of the world.

The geological origin of oil

World oil deposits occur in only a few of the potentially oil-bearing geological provinces. Oil forms and is stored only when an exceptional sequence of events occurs. Oil formation begins with the proliferation of algae, most commonly in shallow oceans. Algal and other organic detritus sinks to the sea-floor where it is covered and sealed by layers of sediment washed into the sea by nearby rivers. These conditions must persist for hundreds of thousands of years. As the sea-floor subsides, partly under the weight of the sediment deposited on it, the organic material is buried and heated by the earth's heat flow. Chemical changes take place converting it into protopetroleums called 'kerogens', some more oil-prone than others.

With the lapse of geological time the kerogen is further heated and converted into oil and gas. The temperature for oil formation generally occurs at depths of 2000–5000 metres and depends on the nature of the kerogen, the duration of its exposure to heat and the temperature reached. Oil may be converted to gas with still more heat and pressure.

The region of oil or gas generation must be in hydraulic communication with an effectively sealed geological structure that can trap and store the oil and gas through geological time. The structure must escape rupture by tectonic and erosional forces that might allow the oil or gas to escape. Most surviving petroleum deposits are in younger geological formations for this reason. Gas and oil usually occur together.

Such a sequence of conditions has understandably occurred only rarely in the history of the earth. Even rarer have been the circumstances of time and place for the prolific generation of oil sufficient to support a major oil-producing province (Campbell 1991, pp. 3–13).

A few giant oil fields

Geologists have identified about 600 potentially petroliferous provinces. Of these, 420 had been explored by the early 1980s. Of these, 240 contained oil and most of the remaining 180 also indicated such possibilities. However, only seven held more than 25 billion barrels and together these contained over two thirds of known world oil supplies. Nearly 90 per cent was located in 6 per cent of these explored provinces (1985 data) (Hall et al. 1986, pp. 189–201).

Most oil is located in a few giant and super-giant fields. Up to 40 per cent of all the oil ever discovered has been found in twenty-five super-giant fields (greater than 10 billion barrels). A further 40 per cent has been found in 338 giant fields (0.5–10 billion barrels). The remaining 20 per cent has been found in over 12 000 smaller fields (Miremadi & Ismail 1993, p. 671).

Discovery rates

Most oil observers say world oil discovery rates have peaked, are declining, and will probably continue to decline. Per year, 25–30 billion barrels were discovered between 1935 and 1970, except during World War II. Between 1970 and the early 1980s the rate dropped to 15–18 billion barrels per year (Hall et al. 1986, p. 190).

A few giant oil fields were discovered in the nineteenth century. The main discovery period began in the 1920s and grew to a peak

Figure 2.5

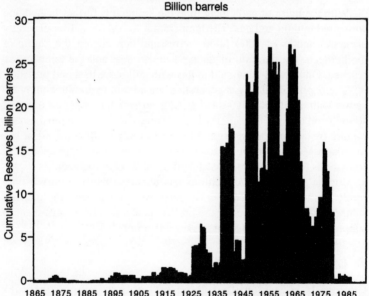

DISCOVERY IN GIANT FIELDS 1865 TO 1985
5 year moving average

Note: Cumulative Reserves attributed to discovery year
Giant Field > 500 billion barrels reserve

The Golden Century of Oil 1950–2050: C. J. Campbell 1991, p. 28.

from 1945 to 1965. There is now a decline that has become extreme since 1980. If the database is to be believed, less oil has been found in new giants since 1980 than at any other time in the twentieth century, (Figure 2.5). The 1980s was an intense period of exploration of great technical sophistication. This suggests the discovery rate in new fields peaked thirty years ago. It needs to be remembered that with Hubbert's analysis the peak rate of discovery occurs first, followed by the peak of reserves, then of production.

Since oil prices collapsed in 1986 the volume of oil discovered in new fields has been less than half of global oil production. The major additions to oil reserves since 1986 have come from revisions to existing producing fields (*Petroleum Gazette* 1990, pp. 6–9). Has the peak of reserves now been reached?

Two thirds of *reported* world oil reserves are in the largest of the oil provinces, the Arabian-Iranian. Between 1987 and 1989 the Big Six producers in this province substantially upgraded their reserves by some 66 per cent or 260 billion barrels, representing a 38 per cent increase in world oil reserves. Such an increase would surely have to include fields in the giant and super-giant classes, or hundreds of smaller fields. The Big Six did not report significant new discoveries to justify these increases. If genuine, they must be attributed mainly to reserve revisions in existing fields. As such, the revisions were extraordinarily large. Further, when all six make such increases simultaneously suspicions are aroused, especially when these are made shortly after the 1986 oil-price slump. It is hard to believe that reserve extensions to existing fields could account for these increases.

C. J. Campbell, in his book *The Golden Century of Oil 1950–2050*, claims that most of these increases are political oil, invented to give an advantage around the Organization of Petroleum Exporting Countries (OPEC) quota-bargaining table and to discourage conservation of and exploration for oil elsewhere (Campbell 1991, pp. 22–4). He has significantly discounted published reserve figures of the Big Six. These countries' statistics are not subject to independent public audit.

Mexico and Venezuela also announced suspect reserve increases at the same time. Both have a history of suspect statistics.

Kuwaiti reserves may have been reduced by uncontrolled flows from wells set alight during the 1991 Gulf War, thereby damaging the reservoirs, but no announcements have been made.

John Grace of Troika Energy Services, Dallas, says FSU reserves of oil and gas may also be overstated. The centralised control of the economy encouraged the petroleum industry to exaggerate finds in the competition for resource allocations from the central government (Grace 1995).

However, the ten years since 1986 have seen the most significant technical advances and cost reductions in the petroleum industry's history, driven by the oil-price collapse in that year. These advances have helped to increase oil yields from reservoirs, a subject that will be discussed later.

The Big Six and the Latin Americans *may* have reassessed their reserves in response to these advances. Even so the increases were very large. Iran and Iraq doubled their reserves while Abu Dhabi increased theirs threefold (Campbell 1991, p. 23). John Shawley, president of BP Developments Australia Ltd, estimated that half of future reserve increases would come from additions to existing fields (*Petroleum Gazette* 1990, pp. 6–9). If this is so then these increases may already be substantially factored into the published reserve figures of the Big Six.

Reported global oil reserves have been around 1000 billion barrels since 1989. Additional oil production from 1993 to 2000 will be about 170 billion barrels (BP 1994). These facts suggest that the global reserves peak, the second Hubbert peak, may have been reached since 1986, or is imminent. Whether this is so should be apparent by 2000 or shortly after. Rubbery statistics prevent a better estimate.

Reserves/Production Ratio, now a misleading statistic

A statistic widely used by the petroleum industry is the Reserves/Production Ratio (R/P). It is calculated by dividing proven reserves by the current production rate to give an index of field life in years. The current world figure is forty-three years. This is a misleading index for the uninformed, particularly as production is now near the peak rate. It disguises the fact that the peak production rate occurs much earlier than the R/P figure implies. Also production continues at a reducing rate for much longer than the R/P 'life' of the resource.

Furthermore, once the Hubbert production peak is passed, both denominator and numerator decrease together. The R/P ratio still shows a sustained life, but obscures the fact that the production rate is continually declining. R/P now conveys a false sense of security to the uninformed. Production does not continue at present near maximum levels to the very last day then drop to zero the next, as the ratio implies.

Why does the industry continue to use such a misleading index? It was not so misleading in the phase rising to the peak of discoveries, when production lagged behind discovery. Then the ratio gives a long 'life' that has some validity. However, the Hubbert approach gives a clearer, more accurate and honest assessment once the statistical base is adequate. It can only be concluded that assessments of the Hubbert kind would create nervousness with shareholders, the stock market and with financiers, and perhaps make companies vulnerable to a takeover. Their credit rating for borrowings may be adversely affected. Governments and the public might take stronger initiatives on conservation measures, on economic reform to reduce oil consumption and promote the use of alternative fuels. Anything is used to disguise the real situation; after all, the industry is in the business of selling its products.

Journalists and politicians in particular seem to be taken in by the R/P ratio, not being aware of the Hubbert curve. But it is an index designed to continue the sense of short-term security — that there is nothing wrong with consuming oil at high rates, that the next generation will probably be just as well off as we are. This is a myth that must be exposed.

Ultimate global production

How much more economically extractable oil will be found? What will it cost to find and develop? What extensions to reserves from existing fields are possible and at what cost? Where will new oil be found? What obstacles exist?

Campbell says qualified authorities have made forty-seven estimates of the world's ultimate oil recovery since 1942. Operations in 1942 were mainly limited to the onshore when a figure of 600 billion barrels was proposed, slightly less than current cumulative consumption. In the 1950s and 1960s estimates grew rapidly on the strength of giant oilfield discovery and with the opening of the offshore, thought to hold great promise. An all-time high estimate of 3550 billion barrels was published in 1969. Since then the trend has been downwards, reflecting the decline in giant discovery and disappointments from many offshore areas. Estimates since 1980 have centred around 2000 billion barrels (Campbell 1991, p. 35).

Since 1980 one third of world oil has come from only twenty-five giant fields, according to BP's Managing Director of Exploration, John Browne. Many are now at the mature stage of their life cycle and have been on stream since the 1970s or earlier. Eight, including the largest, are in the Middle East. Many now require significant new investment to maintain production levels. The world oil situation is moving from a long period of surplus to a period of bare sufficiency (*Petroleum Gazette* 1992).

BP's John Shawley says at least 60 per cent of the world's oil production comes from only thirty-seven fields, each containing over 5 billion barrels. Of these twenty-seven are located in OPEC countries. Of the balance, three are located in the USA, three in Mexico, two in the FSU, one in China and one in the North Sea. Production from most of these fields has peaked, consistent with their producing age, which for many exceeds forty years (*Petroleum Gazette* 1990).

By December 1993, cumulative global production of oil had reached some 735 billion barrels. Proven reserves were reputed to be 1009 billion barrels, a total of 1744 billion barrels. Annual consumption in 1995 is about 23 billion barrels. Cumulative world production and proven reserves to 1993 for the eight major producing regions are shown in Figure 2.6 (BP 1994; *Petroleum Gazette* 1992). The dominant position of the Middle East with some two thirds of oil reserves is starkly apparent. Note that oil production in the USA and FSU/China has already passed the halfway mark for oil discovered so far. The remainder of the world outside the Middle East is passing through this peak in the 1990s. If no more oil was discovered global production would peak, the Hubbert midpoint, about 2000.

What is the scope for discovery of more major petroleum provinces?

Masters, Root and Attanasi of the US Geological Survey say differences in estimates of ultimate recoverable global petroleum resources are narrowing as the core understanding of its geological history consolidates and as exploration has covered the entire world. They say four realms are recognisable where the combination of physical and biological conditions (source rock, reservoir rock, trap, seal and timing) were either favourable or unfavourable in geologic time for generation and entrapment of petroleum. These realms are called the Tethyan, Boreal, South Gondwana and Pacific.

Tethyan realm

About sixty-five per cent of the world's petroleum is associated with this realm. The Tethys was an equatorial seaway between the palaeocontinents of Laurasia (northern) and Gondwanaland (southern). The Mediterranean Sea is its western remnant. The conditions 30 degrees north and south of the equator were ideal for generation of oil. The shallow warm seas were ideal for prolific algae growth, for the formation of limestone traps, and salt dome seals. Tectonic activity also favoured trap formation in the Tethys. This realm embraces the Caribbean, North Africa, the Middle East and Indonesia.

Boreal realm

The Boreal realm is north of the Tethys and comprises the FSU, Europe and north-east America. It contains about twenty-five per cent of the world's petroleum. During Palaeozoic time the land masses of this realm were further south and partly in tropical waters adjacent to the Tethys realm, sharing in the favourable petroleum generating and entrapment conditions there.

Figure 2.6

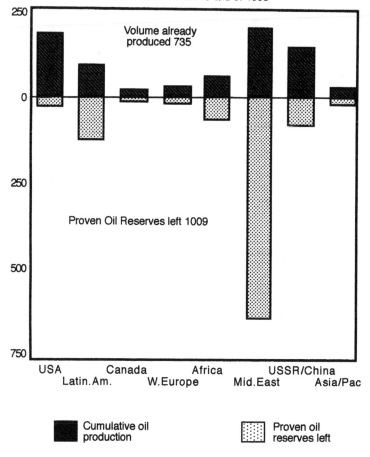

CUMULATIVVE OIL PRODUCTION:
PROVEN OIL RESERVES LEFT

Billions of barrels to end of 1993

Volume already produced 735

Proven Oil Reserves left 1009

USA   Canada   Africa   USSR/China
    Latin.Am.   W.Europe   Mid.East   Asia/Pac

Cumulative oil production

Proven oil reserves left

Sources: Petroleum Gazette AIP 1/1992, p. 17.
BP Statistical Review of World Energy, June 1994

South Gondwana realm

This realm comprises all but the northern parts of Africa and South America as well as Australia and Antarctica. The land of this realm was clustered around Antarctica in unfavourable waters and climate for petroleum generation and entrapment when compared with the Tethys and Boreal realms. Consequently, the South Gondwana realm has only five per cent of global petroleum.

Pacific realm

This realm borders the Pacific Ocean — the Pacific rim. It is a region of active plate tectonics and subduction of oceanic floor under continents. The significant tectonic activity has disrupted whatever petroleum traps that may have formed and held oil. Intense volcanic activity associated with these subducting ocean floors has further limited the survival of significant petroleum resources. This realm has five per cent of world petroleum resources.

Masters et al. are substantially confident that new large oil occurrences (in the order of twenty billion barrels) are unlikely, none have been found in recent decades of intense exploration (Masters et al. 1991). The large petroleum resources of the Middle East are most likely unique.

New oil fields found in the South Gondwana and Pacific realms are likely to be expensive to develop and operate, either because of their anticipated small size or else because of remoteness and difficult conditions. These are the principal reasons why exploration has not yet occurred. They are likely to have low EPRs in comparison with current major producing fields. Political instability has been a barrier in some regions. From commencement of exploration to first production could take up to a decade in new provinces. The financial risk to companies pioneering exploration is extremely high while oil prices remain low, and Middle Eastern countries can produce new oil quickly at a much lower cost.

Ivanhoe and Leckie, oil exploration consultants, say digital seismic surveys have decreased the average finding time required to discover a new basin's five largest fields from fourteen years in the 1940s to six years in the 1970s. Developing production capacity would take additional time. Today's exploration techniques are more sophisticated than ever before. The chances of giant fields escaping early detection are low, especially onshore. They say no new major oil provinces were found during the world's great drilling surge between 1978 and 1986 (Ivanhoe & Leckie 1993).

Some 70 per cent of potential oil provinces had been explored by the early 1980s, as explained earlier. On a pro rata basis discovery of a further 750 billion barrels could be expected from unexplored provinces. But how unique are the Arabian Gulf fields, where half of the oil ever discovered has been found? The earlier discussion on the unique events needed for the generation and storage of oil in nature is of relevance here. If Arabian Gulf oil resources are unique then the above pro-rata figure should be reduced, perhaps by half or more. The 1980s failure to find new major oil provinces tends to support this view.

In 1986 oil prices collapsed to a low of US$10 per barrel when consumption fell following high prices arising from the 1979 Iranian oil crisis. Paul Tempest, director general of the World Petroleum Council, in an address to the Australian Petroleum Exploration Association's (APEA) 1993 Conference, said the price fall had sparked a rapid round of cost-cutting, contract renegotiation and technical innovation in the offshore oil industry (Tempest 1993). There were major changes to offshore platform design, with developments such as tension-leg and floating structures for deep water. (Tension-leg platforms consist of a buoyant hull anchored to the sea-floor by steel tendons.)

Tempest said sub-sea well heads, together with directional and horizontal drilling techniques, have increased the number and range of wells that can be serviced from one platform. These horizontal wells also enable increased recovery of oil-in-place. The innovations have reduced the number of platforms and pipelines to shore that are needed. Together they have reduced offshore costs by well over half since 1986. It has been the most intense period of innovation in the industry's history.

These innovations were also driven by the industry's realisation that the likelihood of finding new giant-category offshore fields had lessened appreciably. Oil exploration therefore began focusing on smaller fields previously classified as marginal (*Petroleum Gazette* 1993).

The cumulative effect of these technical advances and savings has permitted the industry to push into deeper water, to exploit much smaller oil accumulations and more difficult geological structures, despite lower oil prices. BP's John Shawley expects that half the future additions to proven reserves will come from extensions to existing fields through such enhanced production techniques. The remainder would come from newly discovered fields in both producing and unexplored provinces (*Petroleum Gazette* 1990).

Potentially economic oil resources increase both as oil prices increase, and as innovations bring production costs down. More oil can be pumped out from a field before its abandonment. For the offshore the main yield gains from price increases are in the US$15–20 per barrel price range, at higher prices the gains are not as great. There is potential for more yield increases through cost reductions beyond those already achieved since the mid-1980s. Most of the yield gains come with cost reductions of up to thirty per cent (*Petroleum Gazette* 1993). The yield benefit from cost reductions of more than thirty per cent diminishes. The easier innovations with the greatest impact on yield have probably already been made, it becomes much harder to extract the last dregs of oil.

The Bureau of Resource Sciences (BRS) in Canberra reports studies showing enhanced oil recovery can increase Australia's proven reserves by 16 per cent. The processes considered were miscible, alkaline polymer, surfactant and steam flooding, and in-situ combustion. Such developments — especially the last two — would have low EPRs. Miscible flooding with carbon dioxide or ethane was found to have the widest application to Australian oil reservoirs (BRS 1994, p. 14).

However, increased reservoir yields from higher prices implies higher costs and a lower EPR: greater relative energy inputs to produce a barrel of oil. There is also a suggestion that price has a bigger impact on increasing potential resources than do cost reductions. While cost-cutting innovations act to increase EPRs, they are being used to develop otherwise marginal oil fields to the limit of current oil prices, which reduces EPR. Eventually innovations must lose out to a diminishing resource. EPR considerations will ultimately limit the economic additions to reserves from price increases and innovations, an issue few understand.

This is confirmed by Conn and White in *Revolution in Upstream Oil and Gas* which explains the limited commercial success of many such innovations. Very few of these innovations have fundamentally altered the economics and poor financial returns of the exploration and production business, only compensating for low prices and smaller fields. The most dramatic move has been into deep water and harsh areas. But the huge development and production costs for these enormous facilities create difficult economics for most reservoir sizes and well productivities. The technology requirements and size of capital commitment put these projects out of reach for all but a few companies (Conn & White 1994, p. 36).

Saudi Arabia has the world's largest oil field at Ghawar. The producing strata have high permeability, and changes in pumping rate can be monitored for many kilometres. This may limit the potential to increase production by more than 20 per cent using infill drilling due to rapid interference between wells. Thus the possibility of increasing production may be more limited than for many other fields (Kanak & Walker 1989). However, such fields may respond to the new horizontal drilling techniques. The importance of these factors is not clear.

When will oil production peak?

Taking these factors into consideration, a broad assessment of likely ultimate global oil production can be made. Table 2.1 has two estimates. The high estimate assumes the Arabian Gulf petroleum province is not geologically unique; the low estimate does. The high one assumes that all the uncertainties outlined work favourably to increase ultimate production while the opposite is the case for the low estimate. The low estimate assumes Arabian Gulf reported oil reserves are overestimated, while the high estimate does not.

Table 2.1
High and low estimates of ultimate global oil production (billion barrels)

	Low	High
Cumulative production to 1993	740	740
Proven or reputed reserves end 1993	850	1010
Extensions to existing reserves	140	250
New field discoveries	270	500
Totals	**2000**	**2500**

Estimated peak production year 2003–2012 (Hubbert midpoint)

BP's John Browne estimated that ultimate global oil production would reach 2600 billion barrels (*Petroleum Gazette* 1992). Hubbert made two estimates of ultimate global production in 1969. The higher one was 2000 billion barrels (Hubbert 1969, pp. 194–7).

Conn and White estimated undiscovered oil to be 410 billion barrels. They were not clear whether this estimate was exclusively new-field discoveries or included extensions to existing reserves as well. Their estimate by region is shown in Table 2.2, converted from million tonnes of oil to billion barrels.

Table 2.2
Estimate of undiscovered oil (billion barrels)

Commonwealth of Independent States	95
Middle East	117
Asia	51
USA	44
South America	59
Africa	29
Western Europe	15
Total	**410**

Source: Conn & White 1994, from Exhibit 4.8.

The global oil production peak, the Hubbert midpoint, is likely to occur between 2003 and 2012 for these oil consumption and supply scenarios.

Conn and White also estimated the undiscovered natural gas in the world to be equivalent to 718 billion barrels of oil, with over 50 per cent expected from the Commonwealth of Independent States and the Middle East. These two regions already have 70 per cent of global oil and gas reserves.

However, these estimates assume stable, modest economic growth with attendant growth in petroleum consumption to the peak. It assumes no strong conservation or oil substitution initiatives occur sufficient to blunt oil consumption. It also assumes continued political stability in the major oil-producing and consuming regions and that the required investments are affordable and will be made when required.

The world is in the middle of a fifty-year period when production from major oil-producing regions is progressively peaking. The first fossil fuel is going over the hill.

3
Oil: Australia on the Brink

Australia has all three fossil fuels: coal, natural gas and oil. Coal is abundant, natural gas rather less so. But the country is very deficient in oil.

A significant net energy exporter, Australia is one of the few developed nations in this position. All Australia's oil was imported until the early 1970s when the Bass Strait oil and gas fields began producing, together with minor fields in Central and Western Australia. Local oil production has met 70 to 90 per cent of consumption since the mid-1970s.

Local oil production, together with expanding coal exports from the late 1960s, helped cushion the country against the more extreme economic consequences of the two 1970s oil crises. Australia is now the world's largest exporter of coal.

Transport consumes the bulk of Australian oil. Without oil, our cities, towns, farms, industry and mines would quickly grind to a halt. Despite the 1970s oil crises, Australian urban and economic development has continued down a pathway of increased and expensive dependence on oil-powered transport, both absolutely and relative to other nations. We have not pursued energy efficiency with the vigour of other countries. Our present economic difficulties are partly a consequence of these energy-extravagant trends. These issues and the limited prospects for alternative fuels will be discussed in later chapters.

Australian oil production is expected to plunge by 2005, just when world supply and demand is also tightening. World oil production is going 'over the hill'. We will then agonise over more than two decades of folly and the lost opportunities for a more energy-sustainable path. Life will be much harder in the twenty-first century as a consequence.

Production, consumption and trade

Australian energy production and consumption of fuel for 1993–94 is shown in Table 3.1. Oil has the largest consumption share despite being the scarcest indigenous fuel. Coal in Australia is used almost exclusively for power generation and metallurgy, principally the iron and steel industry.

Table 3.1
Energy production and consumption 1993–94 (petajoules)

Source	Production		Consumption	
	PJ	%	PJ	%
Crude oil	1061	12	1502	36
Black coal	4787	53	1197	29
Natural gas	1054	12	733	17
Brown coal	487	5	487	12
Uranium	1293	14		
Renewables	254	3	255	6
LPG	100	1	N/A	N/A
Total	**9036**	**100.0**	**4174**	**100.0**

Source: ABARE 1995, pp. 10, 20, adapted from Tables 1 and 9.

Over 70 per cent of coal production is exported from mines in New South Wales and Queensland. Coal reserves in Tasmania, South and Western Australia are small and produce coal with lower heat value. Brown coal is only mined in Victoria for electricity generation. Natural gas is exported from the North West Shelf in Western Australia. Liquid petroleum is Australia's only significant energy import, as shown in Table 3.2.

Australia's economic and sub economic reserves of both black and brown coal are several hundred times annual production. Natural gas reserves are over seventy times annual production, and increasing. However, half of the natural gas reserves are classified as sub economic, with 75 per cent located off the North West Coast of Western Australia, remote from the main domestic markets (ABARE 1995, p. 22; BRS 1994, p. 13). It is oil that is the critical fossil fuel for Australia.

Table 3.2
Australian energy trade 1993–94 (petajoules)

Source	Exports	Imports	Net imports
Black coal & products	3684		
Uranium	1876		
Crude oil	364	787	423
Natural gas	321		
Petroleum products	169	104	(65)
Total	**6414**	**891**	**358**

Source: ABARE 1995, p. 21, Table 10. Net imports column derived.

History

Commercial oil discovery began at Moonie in Queensland in 1961. The 1960s were a spectacular decade of petroleum discovery which the Australian Institute of Petroleum (AIP) says is unlikely to be repeated (AIP 1992, p. 3).

After Moonie, petroleum was found in Central and Western Australia, followed by the significant Bass Strait fields in 1965. The Western Australian North West Shelf gas discoveries followed in the late 1960s. According to the AIP there has not been a discovery between 1978 and 1992 to equal the Bass Strait Fortescue field, a medium-size field found in 1978. This is despite expenditure of billions of dollars on exploration. However, new exploration theories have been developed and almost every sedimentary basin in Australia is being reviewed (AIP 1992, p. 3).

The nature of source rocks in Australia's sedimentary basins, and the temperatures they have experienced, has favoured formation of the lighter oils and a high proportion of natural gas.

Bass Strait has been the mainstay of Australia's oil self sufficiency since the mid-1970s, supplying 66 per cent of production in 1991. The annual production rate was 220 million barrels by the early 1990s, with cumulative production by then of 3200 million barrels, 87 per cent from Bass Strait (AMEC 1991, pp. 21, 25, 27). We currently consume about 280 million barrels of liquid petroleum products each year, increasing at nearly 1.5 per cent per year.

Bass Strait production peaked in 1986 and is in decline. Enhancements such as infill drilling and development of marginal fields has slowed but not halted the decline.

The size of discoveries in Australia, Canada, the USA and the North Sea has been declining, as shown in Figure 3.1. The largest fields, of course, are always found first. Australia's major discoveries of oil and gas may already have been made.

Figure 3.1

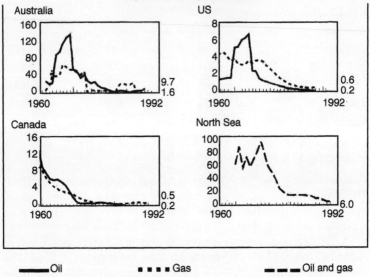

EXPLORATION FIND SIZES DECLINING
Million barrel oil equvalent
(5-year moving average)

——— Oil   ■ ■ ■ ■ Gas   ▬ ▬ ▬ Oil and gas

Sources: Australian Petroleum Exploration Association (APEA); API; Canadian Petroleum Association (CPA); County Natwest Woodmac.

Revolution in Upstream Oil and Gas: Conn and White, 1994, p. 19.

Going over the hill?

Western Australia's North West Shelf and the Bonaparte Shelf in the Timor Sea are becoming the main regions partially replacing Bass Strait. However, these fields are offshore, small and expensive to develop in comparison with the main Bass Strait fields. Their average life is likely to be under the twenty to thirty years expected for the main Bass Strait fields.

The A$1 billion Cossack and Wanaea development on the North West Shelf, launched in 1993, will only produce 233 million barrels of oil, and the LPG stripped from gas, over a maximum life of ten years (AIP 1992; *Oil & Gas Review* 1992; *West Australian* 1993a). This represents less than one year's current Australian crude oil and condensate consumption, yet Wanaea is the largest oil field in Western Australia. Figure 3.2 illustrates the point. It shows forecast Western Australian oil and condensate production from 1994 to 2003. Almost all production will be from offshore fields in the Carnarvon Basin on the North West Shelf. About one third will be condensate from

Figure 3.2

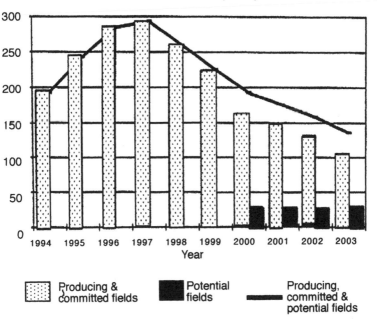

WESTERN AUSTRALIAN OIL AND CONDENSATE PRODUCTION FORECAST 1994–2003

Average oil and condensate production
thousand barrels per day

W.A. Oil and Gas Review: Dept of Resources Development W.A., December, 1994, p. 41.

Woodside's Goodwin and Rankin gas fields. Without new discoveries brought into production immediately, expected oil production will plummet from a 1997 peak — this for the basin that is supposed to be replacing production from Bass Strait!

Note that Figure 3.2 also illustrates that the production rate from these fields is peaking when about half the ultimate production has been produced. Production from the main offshore fields in the Carnarvon Basin began in 1986 and may well end in about 2010.

The BRS published in 1994 estimates of Australian crude oil and condensate production to 2004–5. Condensates are petroleum liquids stripped from natural gas. Figure 3.3 shows these estimates to 2005 together with ABARE's estimate of consumption for the same period. Three production estimates are shown for probabilities of 10, 50 and 90 per cent that at least the indicated level will be reached. The 50 per cent or median estimate is regarded as the most likely outcome; the 10 per cent estimate is possible but less likely.

Figure 3.3

CRUDE OIL AND CONDENSATE
10%, 50%, and 90% chance that supply level will be reached.
Estimated Australian Demand and Supply to 2004–05
Million Barrels

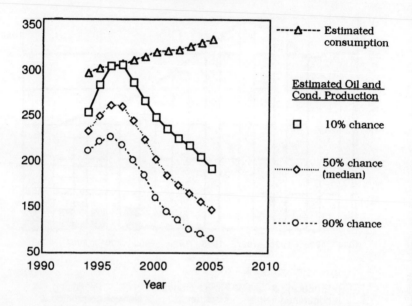

Demand: Data from: Australian Energy Consumption and Production to 2009–10. ABARE 1995, p. 26.

Supply: Data from: Oil & Gas Resources of Australia 1993, BRS 1994, p. 54.

One third of the 2005 production is expected to come from oil fields yet to be discovered. The 50 per cent estimate shows Australian oil self sufficiency plunging from 90 per cent in 1996 to 33 per cent in 2005.

Figure 3.4 translates this data into anticipated import bills using ABARE's estimates of expected international oil prices and exchange rates. Net imports are assumed to be crude oil. This assumption is not strictly correct (see Table 3.2). It overestimates the import bill when applied to early 1990s imports. The relative discrepancy would be less in 2005 when the import volume is expected to be much greater and dominated by crude oil. Australia produces light oils that command a premium price on world markets. Exports of such oil are replaced by cheaper, heavier Middle East crude oils that are needed to produce lubricants and bitumen as refined products. Refined products are both imported and exported as well.

Figure 3.4

POSSIBLE LIQUID PETROLEUM IMPORTS ASSUMED TO BE ALL CRUDE OIL

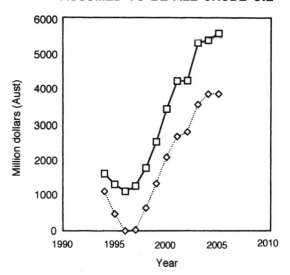

☐ **BRS 50% chance supply estimate, Fig 3.3. Low local supply**

◇ **BRS 10% chance supply estimate, Fig 3.3. High local supply**

Oil prices from: Australian Energy Consumption and Production to 2009–10. ABARE 1995, p. 26.

Net crude oil and petroleum product imports (excluding natural gas) were $291 million in 1991–92 (1992–93 dollars) (ABARE 1993, p. 45). Australia could not afford this level of crude oil imports without severe economic and social distress. The monthly current account deficit has exceeded $A2 billion during the first half of 1995, prompting calls for a harsh Federal budget to reduce the government's deficit. What would be the consequences of another $450 million on the monthly current account deficit? ABARE's estimate of US$19.30 per barrel for oil in 2004–05 is almost certainly too low. The price reached this level in the autumn of 1995. Fluctuating oil prices and currency exchange rates will probably have a bigger impact on the import bill than variations in the volume of oil imports, and Australia will be very vulnerable to supply disruptions from political and other disturbances.

The BRS's 1994 production estimates to 2005 were revised downwards to 55 per cent of their 1990 estimate (BRS 1993, pp. 14–21, 50). This drastic reduction was based on several factors:

- downgraded estimates of oil discoveries in the Bonaparte Basin once regarded as highly prospective but revised downwards because of disappointing drilling results;

- the division of reserves with Indonesia by the Timor Gap Treaty that created a Zone of Cooperation (ZOCA);

- increased rates of oil production from existing wells, which are now expected to run out more rapidly;

- a halving of expected exploration drilling compared with 1990 estimates, affecting the oil discovery rate.

However, a number of discoveries (Elang, Laminaria, Kakatua) were reported in the Timor Gap in 1994. The companies are still evaluating the discoveries which may contain reserves of up to 400 million barrels, still less than two years' consumption (*Bulletin* 1995a).These discoveries were larger than the BRS expected for the Bonaparte Basin, suggesting their expected production rate for 2005 might be on the low side. However, the BRS expects subsequent discoveries to be smaller than the first (BRS 1993, pp. 18–21).

Australian oil and condensate reserves

The BRS's 1993 estimates for Australia's reserves of oil and condensate together with their average estimate for undiscovered reserves are shown in Table 3.3.

Table 3.3
Australian oil & condensate reserves (million barrels)

	Oil	Condensate	Total
Proven, declared commercial	919	641	1560
Recoverable, not yet declared commercial	861	536	1397
Total proven	1780	1177	2957
Undiscovered, average estimate	1800	380	2180
Total proven & undiscovered	**3580**	**1557**	**5137**

Source: BRS 1994, pp. 13, 21, extracted from Tables 2.1 and 3.1.

Total proven reserves of oil and condensate are equivalent to a mere ten years' expected Australian consumption; only six years for oil. Expected undiscovered oil and condensate is only equivalent to about another seven years' consumption. Production of the condensate is dependent on timely development of natural gas fields.

Figure 3.5

AUSTRALIA'S UNDISCOVERED RESOURCES
OF CRUDE OIL AND CONDENSATE

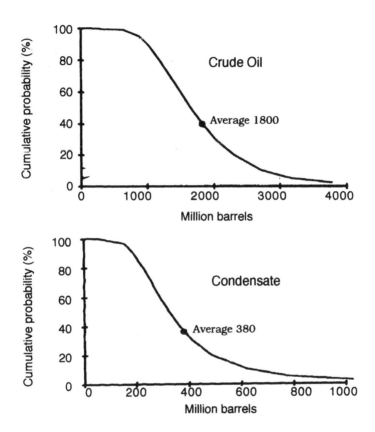

Oil & Gas Resources of Australia 1993, BRS, pp. 17–20.

The BRS's assessment of Australia's undiscovered resources of oil and condensate are shown in figure 3.5. Each point on the curve shows the probability on the vertical axis of discovering at least the amount shown on the horizontal axis. Even expected discoveries with a low probability do not extend the resources by very much.

These are sobering figures considering Australia's dependence on oil for agriculture and powered transport systems.

Australia had produced 3527 million barrels of crude oil up to 1992 (BRS 1994, p. 103). Added to the proven and undiscovered totals (Table 3.3) this comes to a possible ultimate production of about

9000 million barrels. As has already been demonstrated, the peak production rate occurs when about half the ultimate oil has been produced, that is, at about 4500 million barrels. This level will be reached in about 1996 or 1997 (see Figures 3.2 and 3.3). Australian oil production is going over the hill.

Natural gas for vehicles

Natural gas is the only alternative fuel readily available for transport uses. It has some disadvantages, and these will be discussed in chapter 5. A comparison of Australian reserves of natural gas with oil and condensate can put this alternative into perspective. Table 3.4 compares BRS reserve and undiscovered statistics for these fuels. Volumes have been converted to petajoules for comparisons.

Table 3.4
Petroleum reserves in Australia 1992 (petajoules)

Reserve category	Oil & Condensate	Natural gas
Declared commercial	9 300	22 250
Recoverable, not yet declared commercial	8 325	61 250
Totals	17 625	83 500
Undiscovered, average estimate	13 125	18 300
Total	**30 750**	**101 800**
Consumption 1993–94	1 500	730
Production 1992	1 166	1 050

Source: BRS 1994, pp. 13, 17, 19, 20, extracted from Table 2.1, Figures 3.1, 3.4, 3.7.

Gas equalling 10 per cent of the total natural gas quantity was produced before 1992.

About one third of the condensate is associated with natural gas and therefore dependent on concurrent natural gas production. Fifty per cent of natural gas reserves are classified as sub economic (ABARE 1995, p. 22). An example could be the undeveloped Gorgon field on the North West Shelf which is in water up to 300 metres deep.

ABARE expects strong natural gas consumption growth for electric power generation and mineral processing. An 80 per cent consumption increase and a trebling of exports by 2009–10 is forecast (ABARE 1995, pp. 28, 40). Add more for transport to replace oil and the Hubbert peak production for gas could conceivably occur before 2020, an uncomfortably close time.

The cost of gas refuelling outlets to service 30 per cent of light duty engine vehicles would be A$1.3 billion, according to Bruce Moon in a paper, 'Transport Energy in Australia' (1994). His retail outlets were confined to areas with existing gas reticulation. Such an initiative would accelerate the need to develop new gas fields and build a pipeline from the North West Shelf to eastern Australia. Several billion dollars of investment would be needed.

These facts raise a number of important issues.

First, what is the EPR of existing and future gas infrastructure likely to be? How does it compare with current oil production EPR?

Second, the large component of sub economic gas reserves is worrying; what will the EPR be?

Third, what are the consequences for gross national product (GNP) after subtracting the contribution from the energy supply industry?

Fourth, should Australia be exporting gas and using it for power generation or mineral processing to the extent planned?

Finally, what happens beyond 2020?

Exploration and development activity

The BRS says the decline in Australian production and reserves may be arrested to some degree if exploration over the next ten years to 2005 is increased in the producing basins and with greater attention to exploration of other prospective areas (BRS 1993, p. 51). Australia is in a comparable situation to the USA in the early 1970s, and in the North Sea in 1995. The declining size of discoveries in these regions is shown in Figure 3.1, a sure sign that most of the oil has been found.

Australia's comparatively unexplored basins offshore are in the Arafura Sea north of Darwin, while onshore there is the remote Officer Basin north of the Nullarbor Plain. Unexplored areas off the North Queensland coast have the acute problem of proximity to the Great Barrier Reef. Then there are the continental slopes, which are in very deep water.

Part of the Officer Basin was opened for exploration in 1994 by the South Australian government (*Australian Financial Review* 1994c). The basin does not have high prospectivity due to the age of the formations and initial development costs would be high to provide pipeline capacity to the nearest port or refinery. This in turn would require oil discoveries of reasonable size to justify the expenditure. However, onshore oil fields are usually cheaper to develop than those offshore.

Seventy-seven wildcat wells drilled in 1992 discovered less than 10 million barrels of oil — a rather sobering number representing about two weeks' consumption. Australia's prospectivity has a low ranking. Companies have responded by investing increasing amounts overseas — more than 33 per cent of total capital expenditure in 1991–92 (Power 1993). The APEA says 20 to 25 per cent of 1995 exploration expenditure will be overseas (APEA 1995).

The Australian petroleum industry in the five years to 1991–92 had recorded rates of return on investment substantially below those earned by the rest of the minerals sector, according to Peter Power, the chairman of APEA. Financial performance deteriorated in 1991–92 relative to 1990–91 due to weak oil prices (Power 1993). Since late 1993 oil prices have fallen even lower. The poor return and price volatility, of course, inhibit investment.

About A$25 billion will need to be spent finding and developing new oil and gas over the next ten years to 2005 just to maintain the present level of self sufficiency, APEA executive director Dick Wells said in May 1993, $2500 million per year (*West Australian* 1993). This statement was made before BRS reduced its production forecasts for 2005. He later said the 1994 exploration and development program was inadequate to augment this forecast sharp decline in production (*Oil and Gas Australia* 1994).

Wells said that the 1994 offshore exploration program had looked strong when considered against the oil-price outlook and the intense competition for exploration dollars in the Asian region. He said the ability of oil companies to meet their 1994 forecasts would be constrained by the availability of offshore drilling rigs and sluggish oil prices (*West Australian* 1993; *Australian Financial Review* 1994). Later he said companies had reduced their drilling programs due to the drop in oil prices. By spring 1994 these had recovered to around US$18 per barrel.

The BRS 1993 forecast for lower drilling activity is partly a consequence of low oil prices. These will be discussed further in chapter 4.

Despite this discouraging scene, the APEA's survey of projected 1995 exploration and development activity confirmed that 1994 expenditure levels would be maintained, with almost half in the Carnarvon Basin (APEA 1995). Activity in 1994 was slightly up on 1992 and 1993. Expenditure in 1995 was expected to be between $1010 and $1915 million, well below the $2500 million Wells thinks is needed, and 75 per cent would be offshore.

Notwithstanding the 1994 Timor Sea discoveries, the 1995 activity there will be substantially reduced (APEA 1995). The location is in water up to 400 metres deep and is 600 kilometres west of Darwin, the nearest serviced landbase. Development is risky and expensive, especially with current low oil prices. Companies do not seem to be in any hurry to do more than patiently define the extent of their discoveries (*Bulletin* 1995; 1995a). Furthermore, the legality of the Timor Gap

Treaty has been challenged by Portugal in the International Court of Justice at The Hague. The court decided on 30 June 1995 that it did not have jurisdiction, which leaves the issue unresolved.

The per barrel return on investment for new offshore oil developments in Australia, such as the Timor Gap, is higher than can be obtained in Indonesia or Malaysia, is just above that in Vietnam and comparable to returns in the Philippines. The investment returns quickly diminish as the oil price falls below $US20 per barrel, especially for Malaysia and Indonesia. At this price the minimum size profitable field is around thirty to forty million barrels. The returns per barrel do not increase for fields in the 80 to 200 million barrel range (Allinson 1995).

Australian offshore fields are more profitable than in these Asian countries for two reasons. First, their costs are higher due to deeper water, lower well productivity and deeper oil reservoirs. Secondly, these same countries have a much higher tax regime at the well field than does Australia. Consequently a greater percentage of the oil price goes to companies operating in Australia, making smaller discoveries economically viable at a lower oil price (Allinson 1995). The implication for these small Australian fields is a low EPR, without significant cost-cutting innovations. Since the late 1980s, Australian governments have been shifting the tax base on oil from well head to service station pump.

However, this suggests the Australian tax regime may favour development of fields with lower EPRs than the Asian countries. How low and how close to one? What is a prudent lower limit for oilfield EPR? What is the EPR for these oil fields? When is it better to invest in petroleum demand management to reduce oil consumption? The higher well-field tax regime may be a sounder economic policy.

Few analysts think oil prices will rapidly return to the US$20 per barrel achieved early in 1993 (*Australian Financial Review* 1994a). However, political upsets in oil-producing regions and elsewhere could alter this expectation overnight. An end to the recession in Organization of Economic Cooperation and Development (OECD) countries would increase demand. The financial bind that international oil companies and producing nations find themselves in must eventually push up oil prices. Market perceptions could change and the situation is potentially unstable, which also inhibits exploration investment. Chapter 4 discusses these issues.

Woodside Petroleum's 1994 cost-cutting exercise, including the shedding of up to 500 staff, was a direct result of the 1994 drop in oil prices and their negative return on investment since 1983. Woodside's main contract prices for natural gas and LPG are tied to oil prices (*Australian* 1994; *Australian Financial Review* 1994b; *West Australian* 1994). Woodside's staff reduction was mostly in the exploration area.

Ninety-five per cent of Australia's petroleum-producing basins are offshore. The oil accumulations are small, expensive to develop and expensive to operate. The latest ones have short production lives of ten years or less. The peak production rate is often reached within one to three years of start-up. They are vulnerable to low oil prices, and there are more prospective exploration sites elsewhere in the world. Exploration companies are becoming more discriminating — they cannot afford not to be.

Are oil imports the answer?

Could imported oil make up for Australia's declining domestic production? For example, Japan survives almost entirely on imported energy. What must be examined is whether our particular scenario results in a net gain or loss in *energy*. Australia must use energy to produce the goods that are exported in exchange for imported oil.

For coal and natural gas exports the energy cost figure used is the sum of the exported fuel's energy content plus the energy used in producing the fuel and loading it on to a ship (i.e. the sum of all the energy

Figure 3.6

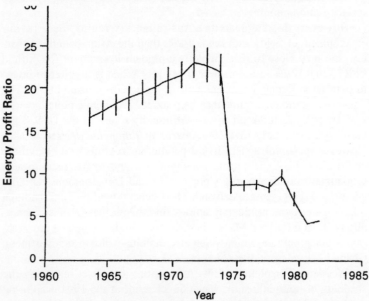

ENERGY PROFIT RATIO FOR US IMPORTED OIL

Note: Vertical bars represent the variation among the different methods for calculation of the energy costs of exports.

Beyond Oil: Gever, Kaufmann, and Vörösmarty, p. 64.

forgone to enable the export to occur). For non fuel exports the energy cost figure is the energy embodied in the production and transport of the exported products. This energy-based exchange allows the calculation of an EPR for imported oil. The EPR is the ratio of energy contained in a dollar's worth of imported fuel divided by the energy contained in, and used to make, a dollar's worth of exports.

The EPR for US oil imports from 1964 to 1982 is shown in Figure 3.6. Since 1986, when oil prices slumped, the EPR for oil imported into the USA would have increased perhaps from 15 to 20. When the EPR of imported oil reaches one there is no point in importing oil as there is no net energy gain. Unless, of course, it is for some limited and highly valued purpose, or for a short period to import petroleum for indispensable needs until structural changes have been implemented to eliminate the need for such imports. But the cost and social stress incurred would be very high.

EPR thus helps define an approximate social and economic price 'ceiling' for the cost of imported oil, and hence the volume of imports that are affordable (Gever et al. 1991, pp. 62–5).

Japan is more efficient than almost any other advanced industrial country at converting energy into high-quality economic dollar value. Since 1950 Japan has survived and even flourished in conventional economic terms. The fixed currency exchange rates of the 1950s and 1960s progressively served to reduce the value of Japan's imports and increase the value of its exports as the productivity of Japanese industry increased. Figure 3.7 shows Japan has the lowest intensity of petrol use per unit of production among industrialised nations. The USA, Canada and Australia have the highest, a reflection of their car dependence.

A key factor in Japan's success was its access, from 1950, to oil production from the Arabian Gulf region. The super-giant fields discovered in the 1940s were coming into production at extremely low cost and with very high EPRs. Virtually all the oil, profit and economic rent from these fields at the time went to major oil companies and governments in Europe, the USA and Japan. This cheap oil was crucial to the rapid post-World War II economic recovery of both Western Europe and Japan. Without it the 1950s and 1960s economic boom could not have happened.

Innovative management practices and some features of Japanese culture also served to make Japan's industry the most effective in the world at converting energy into dollar value. There were no competitors from the Asian region. The generation that experienced World War II had a strong survival motivation and was conscious of Japan's lack of resources. Japan's military machine, industry and nearly all transport except electric trains came to a halt when US forces cut off oil supplies in the first half of 1945.

Figure 3.7

INTENSITY OF PETROL USE PER UNIT OF PRODUCTION

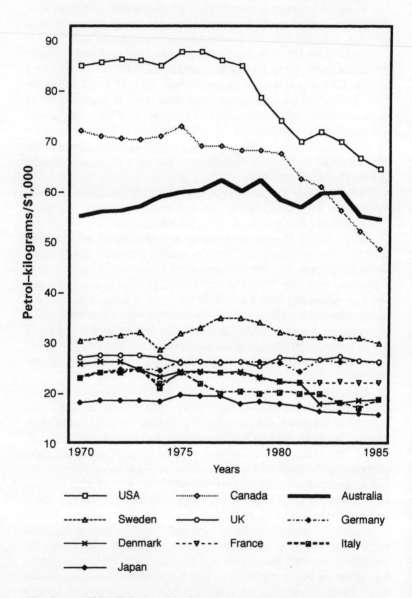

The Energy/GDP Relationship: Bessarab and Newman 1993, Fig. 25.

Fixed international monetary exchange rates up to 1972 gave Japan an ever-increasing competitive advantage. By 1972 the exchange rates no longer reflected the relative economic performance of the nations, a major reason why the fixed-exchange-rate regime ended. Japan's low military expenditure during the cold war kept energy costs low in this area, unlike elsewhere. Japan's energy went into manufacturing and trading excellence. US geopolitical policies until the 1990s favoured Japan as a countervailing force to China and the FSU.

Since the mid-1970s oil-price rises Japanese industry has been restructured to reduce the focus on energy-consuming heavy engineering industries such as shipbuilding and iron and steel manufacture. The emphasis switched to products such as electronic goods. Much of the energy input for the manufacture of these electronic and similar goods occurred in the past during the development of the technology and its supporting infrastructure and information base, thus building the knowledge and skills base. Unlike Australia and the USA, Japan has a much smaller outlay on transport and its infrastructure. Once Japan gained an economic advantage this tended to become self reinforcing.

But eventually the EPR-dictated price ceiling for imported energy will erode Japan's position. The 1986 oil-price falls probably saved Japan temporarily. Now that the cold war has ended, Japan's competitive position relative to other nations is eroding, and conflict with the USA increasing. The 1950s and 1960s were a unique window of opportunity for Japan, an era unlikely to be repeated. Japan is now very vulnerable to the emerging global energy scene and is the major customer for Australia's minerals and energy.

Australia is in a less critical situation regarding liquid petroleum imports than other OECD nations, who nearly all import energy. We are a net exporter of primary energy. However, Australia the USA and Canada have the highest per capita consumption of petrol. Unlike other OECD countries we have increased rather than reduced per capita consumption. Our non-urban transport will always depend on vehicles that carry their own fuel because of distance and low population density. Oil and gas seem to be the only options.

Nevertheless, the EPR-defined price ceiling for oil imports remains. Imports must still be paid for. Nor can we ignore the extreme vulnerability arising from dependence on imported fuel for transport and agriculture. The Middle East is virtually the only supply source. We will be a bit player jostling for Arabian Gulf oil alongside the USA, Europe, China, Japan, Indonesia, India and others.

Australia's vulnerability is the more important issue. Peter Power, managing director of Ampolex Ltd, said in an address to the APEA's 1993 Conference that: 'global trends suggest upward pressure on prices by the end of the decade while Australia's self sufficiency declines, so let's not buy the argument that it's just a trading exercise sell a bit more coal and buy the cheap oil shortfall' (Power 1993).

Beyond oil

Australian oil production is expected to peak by the year 2000, then rapidly decline. A rapid and costly increase in imports will occur when production outside the Middle East also peaks. We are a net energy exporter and are better placed than other developed countries to pay for imports. However, we are one of the highest per capita users of petrol, mostly for road transport. We have car-oriented urban centres, agriculture runs on liquid fuel, industry and commerce depend on it. We are extremely vulnerable.

Chapter 5 will show that natural gas is the only feasible alternative fuel for the transport system Australia has. Other options are excluded mostly on EPR grounds. Even natural gas may be limited in this regard. Half of our natural gas reserves are classed as sub economic and are located 3500 kilometres from the main population centres. What does that mean in EPR terms? How economically effective are these gas resources? We need to know urgently. And the gas reserves are not large.

At present natural gas is used mainly for mineral processing, electricity generation, manufacturing and town gas. The first two uses are expected to increase rapidly by 2010. Add a component for transport and the peaking of our natural gas production comes uncomfortably close, perhaps before 2020.

Australia needs all the oil and gas it has and more to restructure its economy, urban centres, transport systems and agriculture to be able to survive beyond oil. It has taken nearly a century to build what we have. But there are only decades to make the change. Is it wise to burn natural gas so quickly for mineral processing and power generation? Where are our priorities? The present government and business priorities seem to be burn it up as fast as possible.

Australians, government and business are totally unprepared, unaware of the coming impact of declining oil self sufficiency. Such a change in the energy regime is both a threat and an opportunity. It poses an acute need for long-term priorities for natural gas in transport versus other uses. Not all uses can be accommodated. Transport infrastructure has a life of forty years or more and an impact on the pattern of development beyond that. The food system depends on petroleum inputs. Major rebuilding of the non urban road network is imminent. The need to switch fuels presents an opportunity to change direction, to look beyond oil. We do not have much time to change.

4

Unstable Oil Politics

1970s oil crises: challenge and response

In economic history 1973 was a watershed. Oil production had peaked in the USA, the first major producing region in which it did so. The era of declining oil availability with reducing economic effectiveness had begun. For 200 years expanding use of fossil fuels, first coal and then petroleum, had transformed the world. A select few nations were able to achieve unparalleled material prosperity, especially since World War II when oil triumphed over coal. Much of food production has become dependent on fossil-fuel inputs, especially petroleum, necessary to maintain high crop yields to feed a growing world population.

Since 1973 two contradictory trends have emerged. First, the number of nations and people aspiring to share in this fossil-fuel-driven prosperity have been increasing. Second, the peaking of US oil production foreshadowed that this prosperity would not be possible for any nation for long. Societies everywhere will soon be shaking down to a less structured and resource-consuming scale as high-quality energy and other resources diminish. The world may become a better place to live in, or it may not. Issues like ecological sustainability, justice, democracy and equity are becoming sharply focused.

The 1973 oil-supply crisis struck when Middle East oil producers limited supply in order to apply political pressure on European and US governments. The trigger was the Yom Kippur war, where Israel was pitted against Syria and Egypt. The peaking of US oil production and a 6 per cent annual growth in global oil consumption had led to a rapid increase in US oil imports. Thus the USA was for the first time in a politically vulnerable position over oil and OPEC were aware of this. A second crisis occurred in 1979 when the Shah of Iran's government collapsed and was replaced by an Islamic fundamentalist regime hostile to the USA in particular. Oil prices increased tenfold from 1973 to 1980.

Following these oil crises the western world and Japan reduced their dependence on oil from Middle Eastern and other OPEC countries by:

- developing newly discovered fields, for example the North Sea, Alaska, Mexico and minor sources such as Bass Strait in Australia;

- expansion of the use of natural gas in Europe, Japan, the FSU and Australia;

- substituting coal for many uses of oil;

- improving energy end use efficiency (there have been significant fuel-efficiency gains for aircraft, motor vehicles and in many industries); and

- after 1979, establishing strategic reserves of crude oil equal to three months' consumption as a buffer against sudden crises.

Global oil demand fell from 66 million barrels per day in 1979 to 57 million barrels per day in 1985. OPEC production dropped from 31 to 16.5 million barrels per day over the same period (*Petroleum Economist* 1994). Non-OPEC production increased by 10 million barrels per day between 1973 and 1985.

Energy-efficiency initiatives have reduced oil dependence in some countries, as illustrated in Figure 3.7. Note that Australia is the only country that has not improved its economic energy efficiency, a factor contributing to its present economic problems.

These responses became fully effective from the late 1970s. However, the overall EPR of available energy and its economic effectiveness in OECD countries would have been reduced. Rapid expansion of nuclear power stations at the time would have contributed to the EPR decline. The EPRs for a range of energy technologies, including nuclear power, is shown in Table 5.1.

High oil prices from 1973 to 1986 had the effect of transferring wealth from oil consumers to oil producers and the international oil companies. However, the price falls since 1986 have reversed this wealth transfer. Thus the western nations and Japan reduced their dependence on OPEC and Middle East oil by increasing their use of less economically effective fuels. However, the effectiveness of these initiatives is now diminishing. Slower economic growth and rising unemployment in most OECD countries since 1973 are largely an outcome of the 1970s oil crises and the responses to them.

Falling oil consumption in the 1980s undermined OPEC's efforts to maintain oil prices. By 1986 these had fallen from the 1981 high of US$29/barrel to US$10/barrel. Throughout the 1980s Saudi Arabia bore the brunt of falling OPEC production, despite being the world's lowest-cost producer. Saudi Arabia was a producer at the margin, that is, the producer who meets the last increment of demand (Arthur Andersen & Co. 1992). Politics prevailed over economics in OPEC during this period.

Global recession flattened world trade in the early 1980s, induced by the 1979–80 Iranian oil crisis. Many non OECD countries responded to their consequent high indebtedness and capital deficits by resorting to tariffs, quota and payment barriers to limit imports and capital flight.

By the late 1980s export industries in OECD countries had learnt to surmount these barriers by investing in manufacturing in the main target markets. From the mid-1980s this foreign investment increased over four years from US$50 to US$195 billion per annum. The value of goods and services produced worldwide by foreign companies began to exceed the total annual volume of world trade — about US$4200 billion. New markets and centres of technical excellence are arising of regional and global significance, especially in Asia and to a lesser extent in Latin America (Power 1993).

Lower labour costs and welfare overheads, together with fewer environmental and occupational health constraints in these countries would also reduce the impact of declining energy quality (EPR) on the world export industries, competitiveness and profitability. Labour, being closer to subsistence living conditions, would have a lower embodied fossil-fuel content than in OECD countries. Asia has been the centre of this global economic change since 1986. However, the world export industries have solved their 1980s marketing problems by generating development in a region with three times the population of OECD countries. The Asian region now has the potential to generate massive resource consumption of all kinds, including petroleum.

The 1990–91 Gulf War: a transition

By 1990 the USA was again increasing its dependence on Middle East oil as the global supply surplus was narrowing. Iraq's Saddam Hussein invaded Kuwait, triggering the Gulf War.

The loss of Kuwaiti and Iraqi oil production in 1990 enabled Saudi Arabia to restore its production to 8 million barrels per day, near the maximum possible and ending its 1980s role as a producer at the margin. Kuwaiti production was progressively restored during 1992–93. Saudi Arabia is determined to avoid becoming the marginal producer again.

By 1993 global oil production had recovered to 65 million barrels per day and OPEC production had reached 27 million barrels per day. Global demand increases since the mid-1980s have been partly offset by the FSU consumption declines which have been paralleled there by production falls (BP 1994, p. 5). Interest in energy efficiency and conservation has slackened since 1986, and consumption in the Asian region and Arabian Gulf countries has increased by 45 to 50 per cent during the 1980s, a consequence of their rapid economic development.

Consumption has remained comparatively static in most OECD nations over the same period. Industry sources say these global trends are expected to continue, with production reaching 75 million barrels per day by 2000 and OPEC reaching 1979 levels before then. The ending of the 1990s recession in Japan, Europe and elsewhere is anticipated to increase oil use (Arthur Andersen & Co. 1992; *Petroleum Gazette* 1992). By contrast, FSU and Eastern European petroleum consumption and production have both declined significantly since 1989, following the disintegration of the USSR. However, consumption in Eastern Europe is now growing again (Newman 1994).

But there is a price to pay. To meet this expected demand considerable expenditure is required on exploration and development of new oilfields. Increasing expenditure is also necessary to maintain production from ageing oil fields. Low oil prices are inhibiting investment which is below the level needed, a subject discussed later (*Petroleum Gazette* 1992). An investment shortfall has been developing since 1986, as the oil surplus and low prices have inhibited investment.

BP's John Browne said in 1991 that without an imminent and stable oil-price increase to stimulate investment and fund it, supply may not be able to meet demand by the late 1990s. He doubted whether the international oil industry could meet projected world demand of 75 million barrels per day by 2000. Low profit margins are making it uncertain whether needed risk capital of US$250 billion can be raised (*Petroleum Gazette* 1992). Crude-oil prices slumped to US$14 per barrel between September 1993 and February 1994, the lowest since 1986, exacerbating the problem. A recovery to US$16–18 per barrel has occurred since March 1994, but such volatility inhibits investment.

Matthew Simmons, Houston oil industry investment consultant, said the 1994 price collapse was mainly due to the oil futures market losses by a large German industrial firm with contracts for 160 million barrels of oil. The price fell, forcing a sale at a loss, which further depressed oil prices (Simmons 1995).

Simmons believes that oil futures commodity traders have now displaced OPEC as the centre of influence on oil prices. The oil futures market has grown rapidly since 1983. He also said short-term seasonal demand for oil in the first half of 1995 would exceed global supply by up to 2 million barrels per day. Supply is becoming stretched to meet demand, and the system lacks tolerance for any sudden supply shortfall. New oil fields take years to bring into production. He said these market fundamentals always prevail and will ultimately dictate prices. Simmons believes that commodity traders are now underpinning the entire oil industry's behaviour, but with limited understanding of the long-term fundamentals for any commodity, let alone one as complex as oil. Furthermore, they do not have the time to develop that understanding (Simmons 1995).

Bleeding western oil companies

The events since 1973 have devastated western oil companies outside OPEC. The first blow was the loss of oil concessions in the 1970s when the Arabian Gulf countries claimed ownership of the companies' oil production assets. The century-long company-dominated vertical integration of the industry from oil well to service station came to an end. Second, their exclusion from the largest and lowest-cost oil reserves confined them to a few relatively expensive small fields. Finally, their financial base has been eroded since oil prices collapsed in 1986.

The companies are denied access to 73 per cent of global hydrocarbon reserves in the Middle East, the Commonwealth of Independent States (CIS), Mexico and Venezuela. They have limited access to another 16 per cent. Those areas where they do have open or partial access have limited reserves with high and increasing exploration, development and operating costs. Figure 3.1 shows declining discovery sizes for the USA, Canada, Australia and the North Sea. Malaysian discovery sizes have declined from 102 to 31 million barrels since the 1960s, and Indonesia's from 7 to 1.5 million barrels since 1972. Thailand's reserve additions per well by 1985–91 were a quarter of the 1973–78 figure (Conn & White 1994, pp. 52–53).

Twenty-nine large US companies spent US$447 billion on exploration and development from 1982 to 1992 to discover reserve additions worth only US$170 billion, a loss of nearly US$250 billion. Other assets of the companies, such as transport and refining, have also substantially under-performed compared with normal returns expected from such investments. Development, production and overhead costs per barrel of oil equivalent in the USA have doubled since 1974, despite massive restructuring, cost-cutting and mergers on a historically unprecedented scale (Conn & White 1994, pp. 13, 17, 28).

The companies are competing fiercely for concessions from the few countries open to them. It is a sellers' market for concessions and the countries are extracting a high price in taxes and participation in joint ventures, further limiting the companies' revenue base. They are being squeezed between low oil prices and increasing costs in maturing core areas and on the other hand being denied access to low-cost oil-rich areas while competing intensely for concessions in high-cost oil-poor areas (Conn & White 1994, pp. 46, 16).

Those who control the low-cost regions have considerable power over the economics of less advantaged players, primarily the companies. It is to their advantage to see that prices are not so high that they damage economic growth in consuming countries, encourage additional capacity investments by high-cost players, or spur conservation and oil substitution. As North American and European production declines and Middle East producers reclaim market share lost since 1970, the impact of high-cost production areas on the economics of western oil companies will only increase (Conn & White 1994, p. 27). They will continue to bleed even if at a slower rate.

The oil majors, understandably, are reluctant to invest in large infrastructure projects to serve parts of the value chain over which they have no control (Conn & White 1994, p. 65). Arabian Gulf countries, to the extent that they can manipulate the market, can continue such a strategy for some years yet. Historically oil supply has always exceeded demand leading to cut-throat price-cutting in free-market environments. This fact, together with the long-term capital-intensive nature of the industry, has been the powerful driving force behind vertical integration since the days of John D. Rockefeller to stabilise the industry from oil well to petrol pump and reduce financial risk.

Bleeding oil producers

However, this low-priced buyers' market for oil also causes problems for the low-cost producers. Their older producing fields are maturing and need growing investment to sustain production just when low oil prices are limiting incomes, squeezing budgets and compromising past generous subsidies and handouts to a fractious population. OPEC investment required to meet expected demand by 2000 is shown in Table 4.1.

Ismail says 60 per cent of the investment is needed just to sustain production from existing fields at a mature age, that is, those at or beyond their peak production rate. This is the outlay that Indonesia requires just to *limit production decline*. Iranian capacity has gone from 6 million barrels per day in 1979 down to 3.8 million barrels per day. Saudi Arabia needs to add 3 million barrels per day just to increase overall capacity by 2 million barrels per day.

The giant and super-giant oil fields initially have the lowest production costs. Finding and developing costs are low, as are ongoing costs in these initial years. The wells have long lives and usually yield oil readily at a high rate. Oil flow rates per well in OPEC countries vary from 8000 to 12 000 barrels per day for Saudi Arabian, Iranian and Iraqi wells, down to about 250 barrels per day for Indonesia and Venezuelan wells (Stauffer 1994). Costs are allocated over a large quantity of oil. Therefore these wells initially have high EPRs. Expenditure on secondary enhancement to sustain production is not needed for decades until the fields mature and decline begins. Unit costs then start progressively to increase, and EPRs to decline. Consequently there is an inverse relation between the well production rate and unit production costs.

Table 4.1
investments needed for new OPEC capacity

OPEC member	Sustainable capacity Mill. bls/day End 1993	End 2000	Change 1993/2000 Mill. bls/day	Investment needed by 2000 US$bill.	US$/bls/d
Africans	4.6	6.2	1.6	27	16 900
Indonesia	1.4	1	– 0.1	15	—
Venezuela	2.4	3	0.6	16	25 800
Saudi Arabia	8.5	10.0	1.5	17	11 300
Iran	3.8	4.5	0.7	12	17 100
Iraq	2.5	5.0	2.5	8	3 200
Kuwait	2.0	3.0	1	5	5 000
UAE/Qatar	2.7	3.5	0.8	8	10 000
Total OPEC	**27.9**	**36.5**	**8.6**	**108**	**12 500**
M. East OPEC	19.5	26.0	6.5	50	7 700
Other OPEC	8.4	10.5	2.1	58	27 100

Source: adapted from Ismail, 1994, Table 2, p 60. Last column derived.

Oil prices collapsed in 1986 when Saudi Arabia increased production and broke the OPEC cartel. International oil and financial consultant Thomas Stauffer (1994) says this was done for three reasons:

● to discourage conservation;

● to stimulate global economic growth;

◑ to discourage non-OPEC energy supplies of all kinds.

Some commentators say Saudi Arabia wanted to reduce Iraq and Iran's income to undermine their capacity to continue the bloody war between them.

What company would commit billions of dollars to exploration and development in unexplored, risky high-cost regions such as the Falkland Islands off Argentina. Saudi Arabia and Iraq can expand production quickly at low cost and with a pay-back period of months, undercutting any competitors. Stauffer says this has rendered medium-term North Sea, Canadian and US oil development precarious. Australia could be added to the list. He also says low prices have indisputably slowed the pace of drilling because the industry's cash flow is much reduced. This effect, he says, may be as significant as the cost price squeeze in reducing exploration effort.

Low oil prices since 1986 have led to Arabian Gulf and other producing countries going into debt to support the easy habits picked up when oil was dear, such as schemes to make the desert bloom, lavish arms spending and Saudi Arabia's eschewal of income taxes. When money does become available, oil-development projects must compete with other calls on spending. Cuts in public spending programs might follow with attendant political instability (*Economist* 1993). Growing populations are eroding per capita oil income. The Arab billions have gone.

The Saudi Arabian government has run down an estimated US$72 billion of foreign assets to finance its budget and is now borrowing heavily to fund a growing budget deficit. The current account deficit is rising rapidly. It has only paid 20 per cent of the US$65 billion owed to the western allies for aid during the Gulf War. Some Middle East analysts think US$10 billion annually disappears in kickbacks and skimmings. Saudi Arabia has little option but to cut back on subsidies or weapons purchases and to impose income tax. The graduate unemployment rate is 25 per cent and rising. Cut-backs could spark major internal unrest as well as hurt US and European industry (*Petroleum Economist* 1993c). What are the survival chances of the Saudi monarchy? What type of regime might replace it? Would it still be compliant under OECD and US pressure to maintain a low oil price?

Said Aburish, in his book *The Rise and Coming Fall of the House of Saud*, says that since the Gulf War some international bankers are questioning their earlier assumptions about Saudi Arabia. For the first time, UK bankers shied away from participating in a US$4.5 billion loan to the Saudis. They asked, 'Who are we lending to? The government, the State? Or the al-Saud family? There is no difference ... Do you want to predict Saudi's medium term political prospects? I don't'. Aburish says Saudi Arabia's demise was a disaster waiting to happen and would be caused by the corruption of its rulers. He predicts the House of Saud will collapse by 1997 or soon after. 'For the first time ever, the House of Saud's internal, regional and international policies have converged to undermine it.' (*Petroleum Economist* 1994a).

The Gulf War undermined national unity, split the *ulema* — the religious establishment — and drained the country's coffers. Budget cuts raise an awkward question: why should ordinary Saudis tighten their belts unless the 6000 or so princes tighten theirs? The House of Saud may be safe for a time because its domestic opponents are so weak and opposition is still in its infancy and divided. King Fahd is seventy-three, frail and diabetic. In 1992 he laid down that the throne should go to the most suitable family member; he opened up the race. This adds up to a regime starting to fall apart. Change is likely to come from within the ruling family (*Economist* 1995).

A similar financial bind exists in Iran, heightened by the need for large outlays to stop oil production from declining, as shown in Table 4.1 (*Petroleum Economist* 1993). Kuwait is suffering. There is civil war in Algeria; unrest in Nigeria.

A high degree of commonality of interest exists between the Saudi monarchy and the USA. Saudi Arabia is virtually the only western ally in the region. The planned survival of Iraq's Saddam Hussein under UN sanctions in 1991 gave the USA powerful political and military leverage over all Arabian Gulf countries. The Saudis, and Kuwait in particular, depend on US military support for survival. The USA needs assured supplies of cheap oil for short-term economic stability and continuation of its global hegemony.

Some commentators expect the 1990 export embargo imposed on Iraq may be progressively relaxed, commencing in 1995. There are reports that Iraq may be given a limited export quota of half a million barrels per day. A small quota now limits Iraq's potential political gain before increasing global demand forces its production onto the market.

OPEC production quotas will require redistribution when Iraq re-enters the market. Of course each OPEC producer is trying to maximise production to reduce the impact of this redistribution when it comes. Non OPEC, non FSU producers are also maintaining high production levels both to delay the day when Middle East producers will be able to control the market, and for their own revenue and balance of payments reasons. Premature entry of Iraq could lead to a price war and low prices. These would jeopardise both the stability of the Arabian Gulf countries by reducing their income, and the viability of high-cost producers outside the Arabian Gulf.

Russia, China and France are advocating the lifting of Iraqi sanctions. France's Total oil company and Russian interests are keen to invest in Iraqi oil, which has the lowest entry cost of any producer, as shown in Table 4.1 (*Petroleum Economist* 1995).

Some Iranian production capacity has been irretrievably lost through lack of maintenance during the Iran-Iraq war (*Petroleum Economist* 1993). How much of Iraq's production capacity may have been lost for similar reasons? More wars in the Middle East could easily lead to loss of reserves, for example by the torching of oil wells as happened in Kuwait. These factors were not considered by Hubbert. He did not allow for such political uncertainty, nor wider economic factors that could inhibit investment during oil's declining production phase.

Tensions exist between Arabian Gulf countries such as Saudi Arabia and Kuwait who have large oil reserves with low-cost production and small populations, and those with smaller reserves, higher production costs and big populations, such as Iran. The former want to protect oil's long-term share of the energy market by limiting price increases. The latter give higher priority to shorter term income needs. Saudi Arabia is particularly concerned to limit non Middle East exploration, to restrain energy conservation and the use of alternative fuels. The major oil companies have similar motivations, except for the limitation of oil exploration.

Such manoeuvring has helped depress oil prices, especially since 1993. Futures-market speculation and poorly informed commodity traders now significantly influence oil prices, as already explained.

Former Soviet Union, Eastern Europe

Several hundred billion dollars are needed to rehabilitate the deteriorating energy infrastructure in Eastern Europe and the FSU to restore and maintain output from existing oil and gas fields and to find and develop new ones. Many existing wells and pipelines need replacement to arrest and reverse production declines. The military had priority call on investment capital during the cold war years at the expense of investment in basic infrastructure, including the petroleum industry.

FSU production has declined from 12 to under 8 million barrels per day since 1989, but the FSU still exports oil. Consumption has had a corresponding fall as economic activity has declined. Some of the decline is due to ageing oil fields passing their peak, some due to lack of investment both to maintain production from existing fields and for the development of new ones. Some is due to repair work not keeping up with failure rates; some is due to the disorganised state of the economy interrupting production, maintenance and deliveries. Morale is low. Some fields have been permanently damaged by pumping at excessive rates (*Petroleum Economist* 1990; 1991; *Oil & Gas Journal* 1993; 1993a).

Improved economic performance, a less chaotic administration, less corruption, more financial cohesion, as well as enough investment to restore the run-down infrastructure, are needed to stabilise oil production. The Russian Federation has massive quantities of hydrocarbons, especially natural gas, but a large part is inherently very costly to produce. The brightest petroleum future for the FSU republics belongs to Kazakhstan (*Oil & Gas Journal* 1993a). The Russian government estimates that US$2.5–3.5 billion capital spending per year is needed just to maintain the current low oil-production rate (*Oil & Gas Journal* 1995).

Simmons says 1995 FSU oil demand will be half the 1987 level, and the per capita level is now half that of Greece and lower than Portugal's and Mexico's (Simmons 1995). Given the country's size and population it is unlikely that consumption will fall much further. However, to halt falling production will take years and billions of dollars. He says when falling Russian production can no longer match FSU demand, the impact on the narrow margin of spare worldwide production capacity will be sharp.

There is scope for improved energy efficiency in Eastern Europe and the FSU. Massive capital investment is needed — some US$120 billion over two decades for Eastern Europe alone. Eastern European economies are only half as energy efficient as those of the West, while Russian energy consumption per unit of production is triple that of Western European nations (*Petroleum Economist* 1991; *Oil & Gas Journal* 1993). Investment in efficiency could play a key role in stabilising these countries' economies and social structure, and would reduce pollution. Dangerous nuclear power plants could be closed down, as at Chernobyl.

The outcome of the Russian elections in early 1994 has increased the political and economic uncertainty there, but prospects for stabilisation of FSU petroleum production are unlikely in the short term. The economy of the Russian Federation has deteriorated significantly since January 1994, and the Russian Federation's invasion of Chechen early in 1995 has further increased the uncertainty. The risks are inhibiting investment from external sources.

Until the late 1980s the FSU was the world's largest oil producer. However, production has peaked. Huge investment of unknown dimension is needed to restore the oil and gas industry, and expand capacity. Internal financial resources are insufficient. The economic circumstances generating such a restoration would also increase oil consumption to match gains in production, or even to exceed it. Rehabilitation of the Russian economy and petroleum industry must therefore occur together and will take years.

China, Indonesia

Production costs have shot up at China's older fields as expensive recovery techniques are employed to offset production declines. Perversely, China in 1994 decided to allow anyone to own motor cars. The State Council expects to have at least 40 million sedans on the road by 2010 (*Business in China* 1994). China's crude-oil imports may reach 1.3 million barrels per day by 2000, with most coming from the Middle East.

China became an importer of oil during 1993 (*Petroleum Economist* 1993b) as exploration for oil in the South China Sea has not lived up to Chinese expectations. However, China's oil importing has little to do with South China Sea exploration. It is simply due to increasing consumption and declining production from onshore oil fields. Tension is growing between China, Taiwan, Vietnam, the Philippines, Malaysia and Brunei over Spratley Islands sovereignty, an area in the South China Sea thought to contain significant oil resources.

China may have significant oil resources in the Tarim Basin in north-west China. Remoteness at 2500 kilometres from the coast, together with an adverse environment and complex geology, put the Tarim in the high-cost, high-risk category (*China Business Review* 1994). Up to eight years' lead time would be required to produce significant oil from the Tarim, if the oil is there. The indigenous population is mainly Muslim and of Turkic descent; their allegiance to the Chinese has always been weak and is not enhanced by Chinese nuclear weapon testing in the region.

Indonesia is also expected to import oil during the 1990s. Indonesian petroleum product demand has been growing at 7–8 per cent per year. It is doubtful if current production of 1.5 million barrels per day can be maintained until 2000. Not enough new discoveries are scheduled to come on stream to offset the natural decline in mature fields. Consequently President Suharto has taken drastic steps to rein in demand. Fuel subsidies have been eliminated, gasoline and industrial diesel prices have been lifted by 26 per cent and electricity tariffs by 13 per cent (*Petroleum Economist* 1993a). Table 4.1 shows the high cost Indonesia faces to slow production decline.

How will the tightening of global oil supplies impact on the rapidly industrialising Asian countries over the next decade? Are these countries heading down a petroleum-fuelled development path due to collide with available supply early next century? How will this affect global and regional security, not yet reoriented after the ending of the cold war?

An ageing infrastructure

The average age of Very Large Crude Carriers (VLCC) is approaching their twenty year design life (Tempest 1993). The majority of these tankers were built in the mid-1970s. Financially strapped oil companies sold most of their fleets to independents after oil prices collapsed in 1986. Their replacement cost is about US$120 billion. Who will build these ships? Who will provide the finance?

New oil-refinery capacity is needed, especially in the Asian region. The National Oil Companies (NOCs) of the Arabian Gulf aspire to build this capacity and tanker the refined products to consuming countries instead of crude oil, a view expressed by Bahrain National Oil Company's Mohammed Ali (*Oil & Gas Journal* 1994). He advocates joint investment in refineries by producing and consuming countries, that is to move again towards vertical integration of the industry in the interests of security and stability. He favours NOCs building tankers as well. Excess refinery capacity plagued the industry during the 1980s following consumption declines. However Ali says a US$125 billion investment in refineries is needed before 2010.

Up to eight years are needed to reach full production after initial discovery of a new field in a new province. As explorers probe the more remote areas capital costs rise to provide basic infrastructure. The size of discoveries necessary for a viable project increases, and the time from initial exploration to initial production increases.

An oil-price increase is inevitable. The question is when and under what circumstances. The principal reasons are:

- to justify financing new capacity to meet consumption;

- to finance investment to sustain production from ageing fields;

- to finance infrastructure such as tankers, refineries and pipelines;

- to provide cash flow to help fund this investment;

- to meet income needs of the major producing countries.

Will international oil companies be in a fit state, technically and financially, to undertake the task? Not if the present haemorrhaging of their technical and financial capabilities continues for too long. The financial bleeding of oil companies and producing nations cannot continue forever.

BP's John Shawley puts an upper limit of US$30 per barrel for oil (1990 dollars), above which gas and coal would be substituted for oil in static uses and make inroads into transport. Energy conservation would be stimulated. At US$15 per barrel he says oil consumption would increase, conservation and efficiency would decline and the threat of increased product taxation would encourage production constraint on the part of OPEC (*Petroleum Gazette* 1990). Shawley would not have been fully conscious of the EPR or the energy quality significance of his projections.

Since the early 1980s the international oil industry has been consuming its capital. Paul Tempest, the director general of the World Petroleum Council, in an address to the 1993 Conference of APEA, said that:

> the capital stock of the oil industry has been ageing steadily since the early 1980s. The failure in the 1980s to renew production capac-

ities, refineries and transportation systems can be attributed to low rates of return based on assumptions of slack oil market conditions and much lower prices than in the 1970s ... the full capital replacement of the petroleum industry in the 1990s necessary to keep pace with rising global demand would imply investment at a level 50 per cent higher in real terms than in the 1980s. (Tempest 1993)

Capital invested in the energy industry at rising marginal unit cost is capital not available for investment in the rest of the economy that uses the energy and is driven by that energy. Net energy per barrel of oil produced is declining and will decline further.

Petroleum supply for export will inexorably shift to Arabian Gulf countries during the years to 2005, and probably for as long as the oil continues to flow.

A shift of wealth back to Arabian Gulf countries and the companies seems certain in the near future, as happened in the 1970s. How big will the shift be? Too big a shift would plunge the rest of the world into recession, reduce oil consumption and consequently depress oil prices. An unstable outcome is quite possible.

How will these countries be able to use their new economic power? Will they be able to solve ancient enmities between themselves and with the West? Or will the world be facing a series of politically induced oil shocks as the vulnerability of the West is exposed?

The pressure is strong to integrate the industry vertically for the sake of stability, reduced risk, financial strength, coordination, a secure investment climate and the exercise of economic and political power. Will the companies and the major producing nations be able to join forces to do so? Such a development would shift the allegiance of the companies towards the producing nations. Is this a key reason why the US government so resolutely opposes US oil companies seeking concessions in Arabian Gulf countries?

Steps taken by OECD countries to reduce dependence on OPEC oil provided temporary relief that is now fading. The probability of major new discoveries in non OPEC nations is declining given the intensity of exploration effort since the early 1980s (*Petroleum Gazette* 1992).

The easy adjustment options to the 1970s oil crises have been carried out by OECD countries. Fundamental structural change will be needed to respond to the emerging new oil scenario. Its perspective must be a transition towards living without oil. The task will take decades and require the remaining high-quality petroleum resources to carry it out. The longer the companies and the producing nations continue bleeding with low prices and inadequate investment the greater the task becomes to sustain and expand production, and the greater the erosion of the financial and technical resources of the companies needed to carry out the expansion.

Australian self sufficiency is about to decline rapidly just when the global market will tighten and prices rise. Remaining local oil production will make proportionately greater demands on available capital per unit of output. Australia will soon be more dependent on oil imports than at any time since the mid-1970s. It could not be happening at a more unfavourable time. Political instability in the major producing regions could upset the present fragile balance between supply and consumption at any time.

The need for Australia and the world to reduce their dependence on liquid petroleum fuels is urgent, especially for the major use — transport. We are a privileged generation that will witness within a decade the shrinking of its present wealth and mobility. We must have the courage now to explore new ways of living whereby we can all live well, but consume less.

With wisdom and good leadership that inspires people to act, even a better life than we have now may be possible.

5
Alternative Energy Sources

So far, the focus has been mainly on oil developing a theme that its use is approaching a climax. The availability and economic effectiveness of oil have begun to decline in many regions. Numerous alternatives have been advocated and there is now a considerable literature on the subject. Let us now use the methodologies outlined in earlier chapters to scan some of these alternatives to learn which, if any, may be replacements for oil as we have known it.

The energy cost of obtaining free energy, as measured by EPR, will be central to these assessments, as will the other issues raised in chapter 1. These criteria are not well understood and their importance is underestimated. Many on the green and conservationist side of the debate expect more from renewable solar technologies than these are able to deliver. On the other side, the advocates of nuclear power and oil from shale, for example, also fail to understand these criteria.

Yet the latter have the more unrealistic expectations of their technologies than do the conservationists.

Table 5.1 lists the EPR for a number of fuels and technologies based on data up to the early 1980s (Gever et al. 1991, p. 70). A good orthodox summary of the pros and cons of some alternative fuels for transport is outlined in *Alternative Fuels in Australian Transport* published by the Canberra-based Bureau of Transport and Communications Economics (BTCE 1994). The energy-profit-ratio approach leavened with the BTCE's information will enable an assessment to be made of the merit of some alternative energy sources to oil and gas.

Table 5.1
Estimated energy profit ratios for existing fuels and
future technologies

Process	Energy Profit Ratios
Non renewable	
Oil and gas (US domestic well head)	
1940s	Discoveries > 100
1970s	Production 23, Discoveries 8
Coal (mine mouth)	
1950s	80
1970s	30
Oil shale	0.7 to 13.3
Coal liquefaction	0.5 to 8.2
Geopressured gas	1.0 to 5.0
Renewable	
Ethanol (sugar cane)	0.8 to 1.7
Ethanol (corn)	1.3
Ethanol (corn residues)	0.7 to 1.8
Methanol (wood)	2.6
Solar space heat (fossil backup)	
Flatplate collector	1.9
Concentrating collector	1.6
Electricity production	
Coal-fired	
US average	9.0
Western surface coal	
No scrubbers	6.0
Scrubbers	2.5
Hydro power	11.2
Nuclear (lightwater reactor)	4.0
Solar	
Power satellite	2.0
Power tower	4.2
Photovoltaics	1.7 to 10.0
Geothermal	
Liquid dominated	4.0
Hot dry rock	1.9 to 13.0

Source: Gever et al. 1991, p. 70. Data to early 1980s.

Photovoltaics and the solar power tower have made considerable advances since the early 1980s (Gilchrist 1994). Both have the disadvantage of high initial cost, which means a high call on existing high-quality energy supplies during their construction.

The highly centralised global economy constructed since the mid-1830s is crucially dependent upon abundant cheap transport for its functioning. The forty years to 1950 saw oil replace coal as the motive power for rail and ships and the maturing of oil-powered road and air transport. The latter have flourished since World War II, displacing much of rail and sea passenger transport, to become an all-pervasive network holding modern industrial society together. This was the era of abundant cheap oil, with high EPR, obtained from the small number of giant and super-giant oil fields in their prime, an era now passing. The shift of fuel type from coal to electricity, oil and natural gas as more economically effective fuels also contributed to post-World War II prosperity.

Liquid fuels from biomass

There are two possibilities: the alcohols methanol and ethanol obtained from vegetable matter, and vegetable oils.

Alcohols can be obtained by fermentation of sugars and starches. Another alcohol source is lignocellulose — cereal crop residues, sugarcane bagasse, forest residues and sawdust. Up to 10 per cent alcohol is used as a petrol extender in Brazil. There are problems producing and using alcohols in neat form for engines. Adapting existing engines to alcohol fuels reduces engine performance, and engines designed for these fuels are required to get maximum power and fuel performance.

Oils from crops such as rapeseed, sunflower and linseed have been successfully tested in diesel engines. Biodiesel, obtained by reacting oilseeds with methyl alcohol, gives even better performance. Austria is the main user of biodiesel, with 100 service stations selling the fuel obtained from cropping 10 000 hectares of rapeseed. Australia has some 600 000 hectares under oilseed crops, including cotton. Over one million tonnes of vegetable oil is produced per year, about two thirds being from cottonseed. Nevertheless, we are still an importer of these oils for non fuel uses (BTCE 1994, p. 87).

Production of these fuels on a large scale would be in competition with scarce prime agricultural land for food production. Use of crop or forest residues removes valuable organic matter and nutrients needed to maintain soil fertility and structure, subjects discussed in chapter 9. These are serious disadvantages of biofuels.

The cost of these fuels before government excise is two to three times that of petrol or diesel (BTCE 1994). These fuel costs are based on a considerable petroleum input for their production from farm to service station. If the biomass fuels had to substitute for this petroleum input then the cost of alcohols and vegetable oils would skyrocket above the level forecast by the BTCE. This is the fundamental reason for these fuels' low EPR as shown in Table 5.1. Their energy production cost from farm to fuel tank is high.

Technology and experience can improve production efficiency and reduce costs, but the substantial gains needed for their performance to compare with petroleum as we now know it are most unlikely. Alcohols and vegetable oils may play a role in specialist and niche fuel markets, but energy-efficiency considerations will keep their production on a small local scale to minimise transport energy costs for their production and distribution.

Once the right social and economic environment exists for these solar-based energy sources the creative genius of thousands of people will undoubtedly improve their technical and economic performance in ways that best match available local resources and needs. Diversity of form and application is likely to be a feature of their use, but they will never be able to support the transport system we now have. This presupposes a completely different world from today.

Oil from shale

Some shales contain kerogen, the organic precursor to oil discussed in chapter 2. Shale-oil deposits are large, perhaps equalling ultimately recoverable oil (Hall, Cleveland & Kaufmann 1986, pp. 221–8). Canada has large deposits of tar sands in Alberta, sands holding kerogen, like some shales.

By heating the shale in retorts at temperatures up to 500 degrees Celsius a distillate is produced equivalent to crude oil after further refining. Yields of about 90 litres per tonne and upwards are possible. Table 5.1 shows EPRs for shale oil based on pilot plant operation (no commercial operation exists). These EPR figures are almost certainly too high, underestimating costs and environmental impacts associated with the enormous scale of shale projects. The Rundle shale-oil project proposed for Gladstone, Queensland, in the early 1980s illustrates the problems.

Rundle was to produce 250 000 barrels of oil per day, one-third of Australia's 1995 consumption. Mining of up to 1 million tonnes of overburden plus 0.5 million tonnes of shale every day was planned from pits up to 300 metres deep. This was a greater tonnage than was mined each day from all other Queensland mines. The project needed a 500 MW power station, with coalmine, and huge amounts of water. Shale expands on heating, creating immense disposal problems, as the original open pit is too small to receive it and the returned overburden. The shale, the spent shale, the oil and most of the water would contain a vast array of pollutants, not yet fully investigated. The estimated cost of building the plant was never finally established, but in 1981 had reached over A$20 billion and was still rising. The cost of the oil produced was estimated to be far in excess of the US$30 per barrel market price at the time (*Age* 1981; *National Times* 1980).

The cost problem will always remain a stumbling block for shale oil. Oil prices may rise, narrowing the gap between costs and prices, but the same oil price rise forces up production costs and the cost of the oil produced. These costs are mainly related to construction and design, which accelerate most as a result of oil-price increases and push shale oil beyond the reach of economics (*Age* 1981). This has been shale oil's history since the 1920s, illustrating what happens when the EPR of a fuel is near one.

Shale oil is like a mirage that retreats as it is approached. Technical innovations are unlikely ever to overcome these problems because of the overwhelming scale of the operations involved.

Oil from coal

Methods for producing oil from coal were developed in Germany during the 1920s and 1930s and used to produce 100 000 barrels of oil per day during World War II. South Africa also produced oil from coal after economic sanctions were imposed by the United Nations over its apartheid policies. However, politics overrode economics in both these cases. The processes have low EPRs with economic consequences similar to those of shale oil.

Attempts to produce oil from coal on a significant scale would require a massive increase in coalmining and lead to a massive increase in greenhouse gas emissions.

Nuclear energy

Table 5.1 shows the low EPR for nuclear energy — a figure that does not include the significant and as yet unknown future energy costs for decommissioning nuclear power plants, safe disposal of radioactive wastes and guarding forever surplus plutonium with nuclear weapons potential. There is an immense high-technology industry supporting nuclear energy that is largely responsible for the low EPR. It includes research establishments, uranium mines and processing plants, uranium enrichment plants, fuel reprocessing plants, nuclear waste disposal systems and the policing systems needed to guard the entire industry, its products and wastes. The industry is capital- and energy-intensive. There is a considerable high-quality fossil-fuel input needed to support the industry.

A large amount of energy is used to enrich the uranium 235 (U235) isotope content of uranium used in nuclear reactors. U235 as the active component in uranium is too dilute to fission, being only 0.7 per cent of the metal. The supply of high-grade uranium ores is limited and any substantial increase in the use of conventional nuclear power will quickly consume these. Lower grade ores would need to be mined at escalating cost, further reducing the EPR of nuclear energy. To get round this problem breeder reactors have been proposed. In breeder reactors ordinary uranium surrounds the active core where there is a high-density neutron flux from fissioning U235. The neutron flux converts the surrounding uranium to plutonium, which can be used as a reactor fuel like U235. The reactor breeds more nuclear fuel from the uranium than it consumes.

Unfortunately, water cannot be used in the primary cooling loop to remove the heat generated in the core as it absorbs too many of the neutrons needed to produce the plutonium. Liquid sodium is used instead, but it becomes radioactive. The heat absorbed in the primary loop by the sodium is transferred to non radioactive sodium in a secondary loop and then to a steam generator, all to avoid radioactive contamination of generating equipment; water and sodium can react to produce explosive quantities of hydrogen if there are leaks. Virtually all the uranium can be converted to plutonium. Breeder reactors are more dangerous than other nuclear reactors due to the high energy density in their core and the use of sodium and water in the heat transfer loops.

Plutonium is extremely toxic and carcinogenic in very small quantities. It is also suitable for nuclear weapons, although a processing plant is needed to extract the plutonium from the spent fuel from a breeder reactor — a hazardous and expensive operation. Consequently, spent fuel and plutonium must be transported around the world between nuclear power plants and processing plants. Extreme surveillance is needed to prevent toxic and radioactive discharges and to prevent plutonium from falling into the hands of terrorists. Surveillance will be needed for hundreds of years at *continuing high energy cost* long after the power stations have closed down; at best these have a life of forty years. Governments have passed legislation limiting the liability of nuclear power plants in the event of an accident releasing radioactive material. Otherwise insurance premiums would have priced nuclear power out of the electricity market. Instead, the taxpayer has to foot the bill (Hall, Cleveland & Kaufmann 1986, pp. 259–83).

The proposals to cope with this decommissioning and policing problem all have an implicit assumption: the fuels available well into the future will be abundantly available and comparable to the high-quality oil and gas produced since 1945. Nothing could be further from the truth. The viability of nuclear power is heavily dependent on a long-term input of high-quality fossil fuels. As petroleum becomes scarce and expensive so too will the real cost of nuclear energy rise.

Nuclear power stations can only produce electricity. The productive use of that electricity in industry and commerce requires an extensive transport system that cannot be readily and extensively powered by electricity.

Most of the USA's nuclear power stations will need to be decommissioned around 2020. By then the USA will have consumed all its high-quality oil and gas reserves. What a terrible legacy to leave our children and grandchildren.

Hydrogen

Hydrogen has many advantages as a fuel. It is clean-burning, has a high energy content per kilogram, can be safer than petroleum fuels, and has a high energy conversion efficiency in engines. It is the only feasible alternative to petroleum fuels for large passenger aircraft. However, it does occupy a large volume compared with other fluid fuels, and storage tanks need to be large on an equal energy basis. The technology for these applications of hydrogen is reasonably well developed.

However, hydrogen does not occur naturally on the planet; it has to be manufactured. The most likely method is electrolysis of water at an energy conversion efficiency of 75–80 per cent (Reed, Stocker & Newman 1992). This conversion efficiency would not take into account the energy cost of building and maintaining the electrolysis plant and hydrogen storage system. This suggests an EPR of perhaps 5 or 6 for hydrogen when the EPRs for electric power production in table 5.1 are considered. The need to manufacture hydrogen using other energy sources will always handicap hydrogen as a fuel. Hydrogen will have a role to play, but not as a replacement for oil and gas as we have known them.

Natural gas

Australia's natural gas resources were discussed briefly in chapter 3. Another source of gas could be methane extracted from coal seams before they are mined. Methane in coalmines is a hazardous problem in underground mines, but the technology to extract the methane commercially has yet to be developed.

Local natural gas is the only viable alternative fuel we have to replace oil for transport if significant imports of transport fuels are to be avoided.

Natural-gas-powered vehicles have a restricted range imposed by gas tank size, weight and cost. Gas requires fuel tanks four times the volume for diesel to have equal range with equal engine efficiencies. Compressed natural gas (CNG) is stored under high pressure at some 200–250 times atmospheric pressure. Full gas-fuel tanks for trucks are five times heavier than for diesel for a 1500 kilometre range. These constraints of weight and volume are most acute for small vehicles.

Conversion of existing engines to gas leads to some efficiency and performance losses. However, engines purpose built for natural gas will be more efficient than petrol or diesel engines (BTCE 1994, pp. 95–125). A substantial gas distribution network and a large market for such engines is necessary before manufacturers will build them.

There are about 500 000 natural-gas-powered vehicles in the world, mostly in Italy and New Zealand.

The Australian Gas Association (AGA) has a plan for Australia to convert 10 per cent of vehicles to natural gas by 2005. AGA says the refuelling infrastructure required is expected to cost A\$700 million and vehicle conversion A\$400 million, but BTCE considers the latter figure to be too low. The greatest economic gains come from truck conversions with pay-back periods of one to three years depending on diesel fuel prices and distance travelled in a year, based on a gas price of 35 cents per cubic metre. One cubic metre of gas is equivalent to one litre of diesel and about 12 per cent more than petrol. At this price the Commonwealth government would have to forgo excise exceeding A\$6 billion per year if gas were substituted for diesel and petrol (BTCE 1994; Austroads 1994, p. 33).

Some government incentives are required to promote rapid conversion of vehicles to natural gas to make gas suppliers and vehicle owners' investments worthwhile. Such action now would cushion the impact of rising crude-oil imports after 2000.

Forty per cent of world natural gas resources are in the FSU. Another 30 per cent are in Arabian Gulf countries. Australia's share is only 0.3 per cent (BP 1994, p. 18). Thus 70 per cent of the world's gas reserves, along with a similar proportion of oil reserves, are located in a north-south region from the Siberian Arctic Ocean through Kazakhstan to the Arabian Gulf. Like oil, most natural gas is located in a small number of very large gas fields that are usually associated with oil fields. This uneven distribution of natural gas resources is a disadvantage for its widespread global use as a fuel.

Natural gas is more expensive to transport than oil, both by pipeline and by ship. A pipeline can transport five times the energy as oil than it can as gas. Gas must be liquefied at –140 degrees Celsius for transport in special ships that cost two to three times more than equivalent oil tankers. Initial capital costs are very high and are a drain on existing high-quality fuels. Long-term high-volume contracts at stable prices are needed for commercial viability.

Electric vehicles

Independent electrically driven vehicles — those not drawing power from overhead wires — require a storage battery that can be recharged from mains electricity or a similar energy source. There is an energy loss when the battery is charged and again when it is discharged to power vehicle-driving motors. At best such conversion efficiencies are around 70 per cent. Thus 50–60 per cent of the energy used to recharge the battery is lost. This, together with the weight and size of battery needed (governed by the laws of electrochemistry), will always limit the potential of independent electric vehicles. (See Table 5.1 for EPRs of electric power sources and for US oil in its prime.)

Battery technology and performance have advanced considerably since the mid-1970s. Central issues are battery-power-weight ratios and vehicle range. But battery physical and chemical limits will ensure that these vehicles will never match the performance of petroleum-powered vehicles.

Alternative fuels comparable to oil and gas

There are no alternative fuels available, nor in sight, to replace in quality and quantity the highly economic and effective petroleum fuels to which we have had privileged access since the mid-1940s, especially to service transport. Remaining oil's economic effectiveness is diminishing compared with that of the last half century.

Remaining Australian oil and gas must be used to restructure the economy for survival without these fuels, a task that will take decades. There is not enough local petroleum left for the task, especially if too much gas is diverted to export, power generation and metallurgy.

The BTCE, in the *Economics of Alternative Fuels in Australian Transport*, did not appreciate that increases in the real cost of oil automatically feed into the production and distribution costs of all the alternative fuels, increasing their price in real terms as well. Such a lack of understanding of energy economics led the BTCE to have a remarkably complacent attitude to the future availability of petroleum fuels in Australia. BTCE had this to say on the world oil situation:

> There is not expected to be a problem with availability of petroleum fuels until well into the next century (Shell 1993; BP, pers. comm. 1992). As at January 1992, world proven oil reserves were equivalent to 45 years' supply at current production rates of about 60 million barrels per day (Shell 1993). Shell (1993) presents a 'plausible scenario' where 'sufficient additional capacity will come on stream to keep crude oil prices fluctuating between US$15 and US$20 a barrel in real terms over the rest of the decade'. BP sees gasoline and diesel as the major transport fuels for the next 30 years, with no serious availability problems in this period.

> Improved oil recovery rates (Trim, pers. comm., 1992) above the current 50 per cent in the Middle East and 60 per cent in Australia

are also possible, as is utilisation of coal and oil shales to produce synthetic gasoline and diesel. However, the likely cost of oil from shale may be no lower than that of other alternative fuels such as ethanol or methanol. (BTCE 1994 pp. 211–13).

These conclusions of the BTCE must be seriously questioned on the following grounds:

- They ignore the impending Hubbert peaks for oil production and the misleading character of the reserves/profit ratio (R/P) as expressed in the forty-five-year world supply estimate.

- They lack understanding of the broader economic implications for oil of EPR up to the Hubbert peak and beyond, in particular the implications for financing exploration and production in new and existing oil fields beyond the peak.

- They do not appreciate the future for GDP arising from the diminishing economic impact of oil and a change of fuel type.

- They have not taken account of the BRS's lowered Australian oil production forecast, nor recognised the EPR ceiling limiting the affordable price for imports.

- Their failure to understand why shale oil and oil from coal are economically non-viable, limiting the viability of alternative fuels from biomass, and indeed for remaining petroleum.

- Their naivety in believing what major oil companies tell them on availability of future petroleum supplies when they are writing a report on alternative fuels.

- Failure to appreciate the consequences of declining US production up to 2005.

- Failure to realise the scale of the problem facing us.

6

The USA: The End of the Road

The folk wisdom that says you cannot have your cake and eat it too means that a resource once used is not available for other purposes. You can only eat the cake once. US agricultural production has increased significantly over sixty years largely as a consequence of petroleum inputs that have increased yields and labour productivity. But the USA will soon be faced with the difficult choice of allocating oil and gas to industrial agriculture at the expense of other uses in order to feed its own population and maintain food exports. Hitherto all oil and gas uses have been accommodated, but it will no longer be possible to have oil and eat it too.

The global hegemony of the USA is declining. The decline began in the 1970s, when US petroleum production peaked. For sixty years the USA has been the world's greatest economic, military and political power. It has been the major exporter of industrial goods, services and agricultural products. The US dollar is still the global reference currency. The cultural ethos and values of US ruling circles have been and still are dominant in the world.

It is useful to examine the linkages between past US economic dominance and the high-quality energy resources underpinning this hegemony. The declining natural resource base outlined for petroleum in chapter 2 will become critical for the USA over the years to 2010, especially for oil and gas resources. The dominant values and ethos of the USA do not acknowledge a limiting resource base. Rather there is a widespread belief that US resourcefulness and inventiveness can overcome all shortages; that it is possible to have oil and eat it too.

Diminishing high-quality energy resources are eroding these values, and the gap between myth and reality will soon be too great to deny or ignore. The consequences flowing from this cultural and economic crisis will transform the way we all think and act.

This chapter presents a snapshot of a more comprehensive study on the USA described in *Beyond Oil* (Gever et al. 1991). Only salient points are described without the full discussion supporting the authors' arguments. Some key issues and problems are outlined.

The US economy is built around an extensive transport system primarily fuelled by petroleum. Industrial agriculture has over sixty years become dependent on petroleum fuels to power machinery and pumps for irrigation, and to provide fertilisers and agricultural chemicals, the basis of the high production levels now achieved. Industrial agriculture is defined here as the total system from farm to kitchen.

Plastics, synthetic fibres and detergents are other products manufactured from petroleum. The aerospace industry and the military machine are other significant industries generated from high-quality oil and gas. A byproduct from the latter has been information technology, namely computers.

The USA has the world's highest per capita consumption of motor petrol, the highest intensity of petrol use per unit of production and the highest energy-GDP ratio of any developed nation. However, US petrol prices and taxes are the world's lowest, encouraging uses unsustainable in the near term. Many Americans see proposals to increase petrol taxes as an infringement of basic freedoms.

Why sixty years of prosperity?

The ratio of GNP in dollars to energy used is a measure of the overall energy efficiency of the economy. The USA's GNP-energy ratio increased by 78 per cent from 1929 to 1983, half the increase occurring after 1970. However, new technology and improved management practices played a minor part. Gever et al. say that 72 per cent of the increase is attributable to the *change in fuel types* from coal to oil and gas, and coal to electricity. As discussed in chapter 1, oil and gas are 1.3 to 2.45 times as effective as coal in adding dollar value to the US economy. Electricity is 2.6 to 14.3 times as effective. Technology's role has been to bring about this switch of fuel type (Gever et al. 1991, pp. 86–8, 269).

These authors say another 24 per cent of the real GNP-energy ratio increase can be accounted for by declining *direct* use of energy by households. The biggest impacts were during World War II when petrol rationing was in force, and after the 1973 oil crisis, when petrol was again short and car travel reduced. Household consumption patterns explain 57 per cent of the variation in real GNP-energy ratios among nations (Gever et al. 1991, p. 90).

Post-World War II GNP-energy ratio increases for Germany, the UK, France and Japan have similar explanations (Gever et al. 1991, p. xxxv).

The increased wealth generated by high-quality petroleum made affordable the enormous diversion of resources supporting the military buildup of the cold war, conspicuous expression of US hegemony. Depleting petroleum resources were a major reason for the end of the cold war, as no nation could afford it any more — a classic example showing how extreme competition leads to resource exhaustion.

Other US resources are declining in quality. For example, the copper content of ores has declined from 2.5 per cent in 1910 to 0.5 per cent in 1980. Chilean ores have 1.5 per cent copper, and Chile is a major world supplier. The energy cost required to extract a metal from ore increases as the ore grade decreases — quite steeply for low-grade ores (Gever et al. 1991, pp. 43–4). The iron content of US iron ore has dropped from 60 to 25 per cent this century. Technology has improved energy extraction efficiency over the years. As ore grades decline, energy-efficiency gains through technology and better management are eventually overwhelmed by the sheer volume of ore to be mined and processed. The energy input required increases dramatically, as do environmental and waste disposal problems.

A decline in the energy production efficiency for non renewable resources is understandable. Similar declines are occurring for many renewable resources. For example, the US fish catch, measured in energy value of edible protein per unit of energy used by fishermen, has halved in the twenty years to the mid-1980s (Gever et al. 1991, pp. 45–6). Overfishing is an important reason; declining fish stocks the main cause.

Agriculture; a cornucopia?

US agriculture has had three development phases. The expansionist phase ended in about 1920 when 390 million acres (158 million hectares) were under cultivation, not greatly different from the area farmed now.

The intensification phase began in the 1930s and continued into the 1970s. Between 1945 and 1970 per acre US corn yield rose from 34 to 81 bushels (from 3 to 7.3 cubic metres per hectare) and total corn production grew 240 per cent. However, on-farm energy costs per bushel rose 51 per cent (Gever et al. 1991, pp. 47–8). The increased yields needed higher energy inputs, mainly petroleum products. Table 6.1 shows indices of on-farm crop production and energy input together with indices of output per unit energy expended, published by the US Department of Agriculture (USDA).

Table 6.1
USDA Crop output index; on-farm energy use index,
1940–79 (1968 = 100)

Year	Output index	Energy index	Output/ energy	Output/ energy ratio 1940 = 100
1940	65	21	3.1	100
1950	76	53	1.43	48
1960	90	69	1.30	42
1970	97	106	0.91	29
1979	140	172	0.81	26

Source: Gever et al. 1991, p. 155. Data selected from Figure 5.1; last column added and derived from the third.

An eightfold increase in energy input was needed to double crop output arising from hybridisation of crop species. These energy inputs came mainly via farm machinery, fertilisers, pesticides and irrigation pumping.

By 1970–78, 50 per cent more energy was needed to grow 30 per cent more crop. The *saturation phase* had begun. Biological and soil limits were being reached, as shown in Figure 6.1. Now more energy input produces negligible yield increases, some say even causing damage to soil organic matter and structure.

The USDA estimates that 23 per cent of US crop land suffers erosion rates greater than is considered 'tolerable', defined in a complicated way for factors such as absolute soil loss, soil formation rates, the value of crops, and others. The usefulness of this definition is in dispute, but not the fact of erosion. The scale and future implications of erosion are in dispute, and estimates vary widely. Soil erosion has been a problem since sedentary agriculture began 10 000 years ago, but is intensified by mechanised tillage techniques. Farmland erosion is again comparable to the dust-bowl of the 1930s, portrayed by Steinbeck in his novel 'Grapes of Wrath'.

Taking crops off fields removes nutrients. Manure and crop residues may be returned, but they do not contain all the original nutrients. The mere act of continuous mechanised tillage compacts the subsoil and reduces the soil's organic matter, critical for retaining moisture and resisting erosion. Commercial fertiliser may replace lost nutrients but cannot replace topsoil. Synthetic fertilisers are significantly less effective on soils lacking some humus. Humus holds fertilisers and moisture in the soil, supporting beneficial populations of micro-organisms and invertebrate life forms. However, fertilisers also

Figure 6.1

INDEX OF AGRICULTURAL OUTPUT (1957–59 = 100) VERSUS ENERGY INPUT 1920 TO 1980

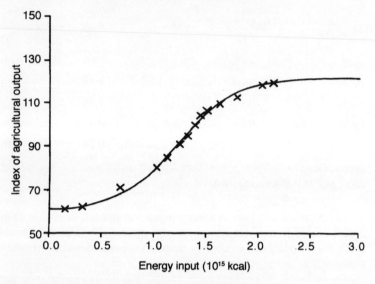

Energy input (10^{15} kcal)

Beyond Oil: Gever, Kaufmann, and Vörösmarty, p. 52.

promote microbial degradation of humus, thus increasing the need for fertilisers. Without humus, fertilisers are likely to be washed away, and increased water may be needed. The threat of erosion is increased, and a vicious cycle can set in. Nutrient enrichment of water bodies follows with consequent damaging algal blooms and degradation of aquatic environments (Gever et al. 1991, pp. 159–66). Attempts to offset soil degradation by using more fertilisers alone can intensify the problems.

Twelve per cent of US crop land is irrigated and accounts for 25 per cent of the value of crops produced. Wheat and sorghum yields are increased fourfold over unirrigated fields. Higher value, higher yielding crops can be grown with irrigation. There are heavy federal subsidies for irrigated agriculture in the western USA. The Olgallala aquifer containing fossil ground water extends from the Canadian border through the US midwest into northern Texas. The water is used extensively for irrigation, industry and town supply. The aquifer is not recharged from rain; the water is being mined. Irrigation from the aquifer can be expanded in Nebraska, but in neighbouring Kansas irrigation water will be exhausted for 75 per cent of existing crop land by 2025. Farmers will have to switch from irrigated corn to lower yielding and lower value dryland wheat. As water levels fall, pumping costs rise.

Diet and oil

About 35 per cent of the average US diet, in calories, consists of animal products such as red meat, poultry, fish, eggs, dairy products and animal fats. Almost 60 per cent of these animal foods are derived from crops harvested to feed animals, not from unimproved pasture or range-lands. For example, 85–90 per cent of the US corn crop used domestically is fed to animals.

It takes almost 11 000 kilocalaries of crops to produce the 700 kilocalories of crop-fed animal products in the average daily diet. Much of this inefficiency stems from a US fondness for beef. Cattle are ruminant animals whose energy conversion ratio of grain or grass to meat is about five times poorer than for chickens or pigs. Much of the impetus for the heavy use of fertilisers, irrigation and pesticides for crops in the US comes, then, from consumer preferences for animal products (Gever et al. 1991, pp. 170–71).

About 4 per cent of the US energy budget is used on the farm to actually grow food. Ten to 13 per cent is used between the farm gate and dinner plate to transport, process, package, cook, freeze, store and distribute food. Four million people work on farms; another 18 million work in the rest of the industrial agricultural system beyond the farm gate. Off-farm energy use increased by 85 per cent between 1950 and 1970, not including home energy use, yet food consumption in kilocalories only increased 40 per cent. Food is now transported thousands of kilometres and can undergo lengthy refrigerated storage to ensure that seasonally grown foods are always available. The US agricultural energy budget from 1940 to 1970 shown in Table 6.2 illustrates the pattern. In the same period there was a fivefold reduction in on-farm labour and a consequent decay of rural towns and communities.

Table 6.2
US agricultural energy budget on-farm and off-farm 1940 to 1970 (trillion kilocalaries)

	1940	1950	1960	1970
On-farm	125	303	374	526
Processing industry	286	454	571	842
Commercial & home	275	377	495	804
Total	**686**	**1134**	**1440**	**2172**

Data from: Beyond Oil: Gever, Kaufmann, Skole and Vörösmarty, p. 174.

Direct energy use was the largest component of on-farm energy use followed by energy embodied in machinery and fertilisers. Energy used for processing and transport was the largest component of energy used in the food processing industry, with transport increasing its share of the total over the thirty year period. Homes consumed the largest component of energy used in the commercial home sector.

Altered consumer food preferences away from grain-fed animal products are the key to improving the energy efficiency of US industrial agriculture.

Food prospects to 2025

The consequences of the declining energy resource base for US industrial agriculture for the period 1985 to 2025 is explored in a model developed by Gever et al. at the Complex Systems Research Center, University of New Hampshire (Gever et al. 1991, pp. 177–215). The issues raised make it worthwhile outlining the work in some detail.

The model catered for factors such as population, diet level and type, USDA-expected agricultural exports, crop-yield curves related to energy input, energy input as percentages of the US energy budget, expected US energy budget, soil degradation forecasts, technology such as genetic engineering, and limitations on land availability. Inputs and outputs were measured in energy units. The crop-yield outputs allowed for both technological advances and soil degradation as opposing factors. The model assumed a constant diet in calories. It was verified against the historical record from 1940 to 1979.

A number of different scenarios were modelled over a range of values for the factors considered. The low and moderate resource quality cases refer to degrees of soil degradation and technology that can affect crop output. The *moderate resource quality* scenario extrapolates current rates of land degradation and technological advancement. The *low resource quality* scenario assumes technology will not improve crop output efficiency and that land degradation is more serious than most people believe. Total demand is domestic plus exports. The model assumes the economic system will continue to function in the way described by neoclassical economic theory — that there will be no major political or economic upsets.

One model run had on-farm energy use capped at three levels (2.5, 5.0 and 7.5 per cent of the US energy budget), kept the land farm limited to the current level of 350 million acres (140 million hectares) for each of low and moderate resource quality. Potential unused agricultural land is of marginal quality or else unimproved grazing land, or forested. This land's existing uses would be sacrificed and would have poor energy efficiency in crop production if used for agriculture. The model assumed no change to the US diet with its high grain-fed animal product component.

All cases showed reduced crop production in years 2000 and 2025 with the greatest reduction for scenarios with the lowest energy input to agriculture. Both the moderate and low resource quality scenarios show there will be progressive decline in US agricultural exports. The low resource quality scenario suggests, for the assumed conditions, that sometime after 2010 the USA could have difficulty feeding its own population, given the present diet high in animal products.

'High-tech' scenarios were modelled as well. Innovations, such as genetic engineering, were channelled into maximising yields while leaving intact the current custom of applying many energy-based inputs. 'Soft path' scenarios were also modelled. These involved more sophisticated farm-management practices and enhanced erosion-control measures, but particularly reduced energy inputs in the form of fertilisers and pesticides that reduced crop yields by 12 per cent by 2000. However, farm costs were reduced more than income and farmers were better off. Innovations still had a role in the 'soft path'.

The 'soft' and 'high-tech' paths in the model had similar outcomes to 2005, but then the soft path gains on the high-tech path, especially for exports. The high-tech path runs into the 5 per cent cap on energy use. The soft path uses 50 per cent less on farm fuel than the high-tech path, only 2.7 per cent of total US energy use in 2025. It would seem that improved crop strains unaccompanied by structural changes in farming practices solve nothing. The soft path requires a reduction in off-farm energy use and above all a reduction in animal products in the US diet to accommodate the reduced crop yields and maintain export levels (Gever et al. 1991, pp. 212–13). US food exports in 1981 offset half of the dollar cost of imported oil (Gever et al. 1991, p. 29).

US food exports play an important part in feeding the world and offsetting drought-induced food shortages. The USA provides more than three quarters of the corn and soybeans, over 40 per cent of the wheat and nearly a quarter of the rice traded on world markets (Gever et al. 1991, p. 148).

Coal, the most likely successor to US oil and gas, is almost useless for direct use in agriculture. As US oil and gas supplies shrink, a higher proportion of these fuels, even under the soft path, will need to be diverted to industrial agriculture to feed the population and continue exports to pay for the oil imports. This diversion can only be at the expense of other uses of oil and gas such as transport. Again, it needs to be remembered that EPR considerations will limit the amount of oil that the USA can import.

In the prologue to the second edition of *Beyond Oil* the authors say that ten years' more data and research since the original study was made has reinforced their claim that US agriculture has entered a period of saturation (Gever et al. 1991, p. xxxii). They saw no reason to change their mid-1980s conclusions.

The US Congress in 1995 will enact five-yearly budget legislation for the US Department of Agriculture. It could reduce the US$62 billion budget by one third. The budget includes export-support subsidies to US farmers, the bane of Australian farmers. Some US farmers have begun adopting more organic, low-tillage practices to reduce erosion, build up soil humus and reduce costs. However, some features of current farm policy and funding conflict with the objectives of sustainable agriculture. For instance, to remain eligible under a major commodity price support program, a farmer must persist with monoculture. It is in his financial interests to apply large amounts of fertilisers and pesticides (*Science* 1995).

The farm-subsidy program would be impeding the changes needed in US agriculture and dietary habits.

Major changes to US agriculture and eating habits are imminent with consequences for the world and those countries now dependent on imported food.

Fuel supply limits wealth

A model of the US economy was also developed by the *Beyond Oil* authors at the University of New Hampshire's Complex Systems Research Center (Gever et al. 1991, pp. 111–46). In this model, the quantity of available fuel and the efficiency with which it is used determine the quantity of goods and services producible, thus linking industrial production to the resource base that increasingly limits it. The model simulates the output that could be achieved if all the fuel physically available were used. It is assumed that non fuel resources will always be adequate and that no radical structural changes to the economy occur. It is also assumed that internal conditions never limit production, the issues of principal concern to neoclassical economic theory.

The model assumed that *total* US energy supplies would not be greatly different in 2025 from the 1982 level. However, coal increased nearly threefold to replace oil and gas, while hydro, nuclear and wood showed little change from an already low level. Oil imports were *assumed* to rise from the present 12 per cent of world production to 15 per cent by 2010, declining to 13 per cent by 2025 due to increasing competition for a shrinking global supply. On this basis oil and gas consumption in 2025 was *one quarter* of the 1985 level, almost all of it imported. The soft path simulation for US agriculture discussed earlier used 2.7 per cent of total US energy in 2025 on the farm, half the 1985 percentage. This suggests a much higher percentage of available oil and gas would need to be diverted to agriculture in 2025 than in 1985.

The authors compared their model with another widely used economic model in the USA, that developed by Data Resources Inc.

(DRI) of Massachusetts. It is in the mould of neoclassical economic theory and no doubt is similar to the Industry Commission's ORANI model of the Australian economy. The DRI model simulates the internal working of the US economy, but assumes external conditions such as resource availability and quality are not limiting, that resources will be available when needed. The DRI model, and others like it, have some limited use for short-term forecasting, say up to five years ahead. Fundamental changes in the resource base are not usually significant over such a period. But even this forecasting claim for these models is now under challenge (Lewin 1993).

These shortcomings are too large to ignore for forecasts twenty or thirty years ahead. By contrast, the energy- and resource-constrained model of Gever et al. is of limited use for short-term forecasting. It is best suited to evaluating longer term impacts of changing external resource quality and availability. This is shown in Figure 6.2 which compares the DRI projection of US domestic oil and gas production with the Hubbert projection. The DRI projection is clearly unrealistic.

Figure 6.2

AMOUNT OF DOMESTIC OIL AND GAS THE DRI MODEL ASSUMES WILL BE PRODUCED VERSUS THE HUBBERT PROJECTION OF OIL AND GAS PRODUCTION

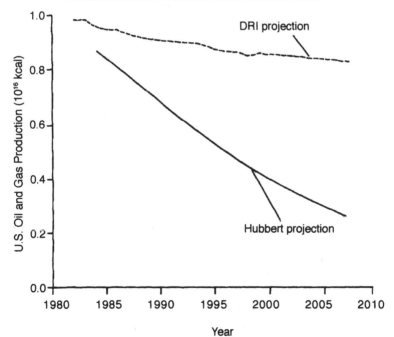

Beyond Oil: Gever, Kaufmann, and Vörösmarty, p. 116.

Figure 6.3 shows the reference scenario for real per capita GNP (1972 dollars) together with the impact of indigenous oil and gas supply projections 25 per cent above and below Hubbert's. The reference scenario is a middle-of-the-road pass based on current economic expectations. Even the opening up of US offshore areas currently closed to oil exploration and development will not make that much difference.

The three profiles are similar. All show a slowing down of per capita GNP growth from the mid-1990s followed by a rapid decline from about 2000. This is understandable considering the declining quantity and EPR of oil and gas and their greater economic effectiveness compared with coal, the fuel type argument of chapter 1.

Other scenarios modelled examined the impact of varying the level of imported oil, nuclear power, alternative electricity, passive solar heat, biomass and population. All showed a similar pattern and timing of the decline of GNP per capita. That US per capita GNP will soon decline therefore seems to be a robust conclusion.

Figure 6.3

WHAT HAPPENS IF DOMESTIC PETROLEUM PRODUCTION VARIES FROM THE HUBBERT CURVE?

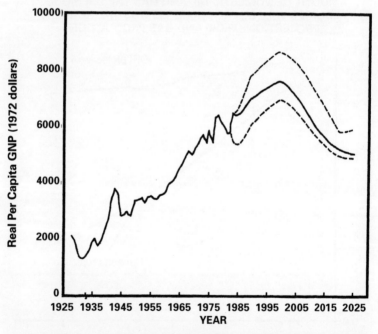

Note: Solid line is historical data and the reference scenario. Dotted lines represent the per capita GNP if Hubbert curves underestimate (upper line) or overestimate (lower line) domestic production.

Beyond Oil: Gever, Kaufmann, and Vörösmarty, p. 125.

The value of the US dollar relative to the German mark and Japanese yen has fallen significantly since late 1994. Economic journalists talk of the US dollar ceasing to be a reference currency. Does this already reflect the impact of deteriorating US energy quality and supply? The fraction of US GNP attributable to natural resource extraction increased from 4 to 10 per cent from 1975 to 1985 (Gever et al. 1991, p. 101). The model reference scenario for energy extraction shows the trend continuing to 2025, as shown in Figure 6.4. GNP is becoming an even more unsatisfactory measure of economic welfare. The effort needed to obtain lower quality fuels should not be included in measurements of *useful* goods and services.

Aggregate labour productivity (real GDP per worker), real weekly wages in US manufacturing industry and real family income have all stopped growing or have declined slightly since 1973, the year US oil

Figure 6.4
**THE FRACTION OF PER CAPITA GNP ACCOUNTED
FOR BY ENERGY EXTRACTION**

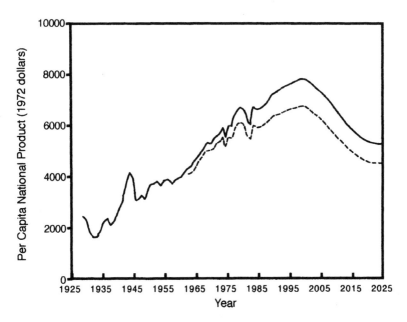

Note: Solid line is historical data and the reference scenario. Dotted line represents the per capita 'non fuel national product' — per capita GNP minus fuel extraction activities.

Beyond Oil: Gever, Kaufmann, and Vörösmarty, p. 141.

production peaked (Gever et al. 1991, pp. xxxvi-xl). Kaufmann, in the prologue to *Beyond Oil*, says the combination of resource depletion and a tight link between economic activity and energy use has already ended a century of rising per capita standards of living, population, and leisure time.

Urban car travel dominates most US cities, as it does in Australia. The consequent low-density urban pattern, the so called 'edge cities', are almost totally dependent on the private motor car. The USA has more than 200 such cities containing two thirds of the country's office facilities. Eighty per cent have been built in the last twenty years. They seldom reach densities to justify any public transport other than a bus. The private motor car dominates (*Petroleum Gazette* 1994). Los Angeles, Denver and Houston are the most conspicuous examples.

US car makers have reported a steep decline in sales since January 1995. The weak sales sent analysts searching for reasons why the industry's sales are slowing more strongly than the economy as a whole (*Australian Financial Review* 1995). The pinch is becoming real.

Private cars will lose out to agriculture and other more essential commercial transport dependent on petroleum fuels. What will happen to these cities and the people who live in them? How fairly will the shrinking wealth be distributed?

Thirty-seven per cent of global air travellers are on US domestic routes, some 410 million people in 1991 (Aerospace Industries Association of America 1992). The world's airlines are expected to make a small profit in 1995 after losing US$16 billion in the previous five years. Annual passenger growth of over 5 per cent is needed for two years to soak up excess capacity (*Australian* 1994c).

Boeing manufactures 60 per cent of all jetliners and had to cut back production by 40 per cent during 1993 and 1994. The worst may not be over (*Australian* 1995). The smaller and newer second-tier airlines in the US have fleets whose average age is well over twenty years. These airlines have increasing difficulty keeping their ageing fleets serviceable and in the air, an issue worrying both Boeing and the Washington General Accounting Office (*Australian Financial Review* 1994f).

Figure 6.3 shows US per capita GNP declining within ten years. Such a decline will certainly shrink the number of US citizens who can afford air travel. A progressive contraction of commercial passenger aviation is implied. The consequences would have global repercussions. It would force airlines everywhere to reassess their traffic projections and forecasting methods. The International Air Transport Association expects a 3.5-fold increase in the number of people flying in the Asia-Pacific region by 2010 (*Australian* 1994a). How realistic are these growth projections? What does this mean for Sydney's second airport at Badgery's Creek and the future of privatised airports and of Qantas? The implications for the future of the tourist and hospitality industries are enormous. The consequences of these trends are already appearing. US manufacturing and some service industries are shifting to lower waged areas like Mexico where the embodied energy of labour is lower. Aaron Bernstein in *Business Week* reported that a June 1995 US Labor Department survey showed real employee compensation actually declining in recent years. Unlike in the 1980s, these trends are now extending into the white-collar area of engineers and computer programmers. He says with inflation-adjusted incomes advancing at half the pace of previous economic upturns consumers are cutting back on everything from cars to airline tickets. He reports Joseph Carson, the chief economist at Dean Witter, Discover & Co., as saying that 'this is the weakest consumption cycle of the postwar period which is largely a reflection of the wage slowdown' (*Australian Financial Review* 1995b).

Detroit car makers, Bernstein says, worry that the average family cannot afford their products any more. Despite productivity increases, a weak US dollar and corporate profits at a forty-five-year high, US companies are still slashing costs as if the recession never ended, shedding jobs and cutting wages. An unnerving question is starting to creep into the discussion: are we simply in the middle of a specially long and wrenching transition, or have structural changes in the economy severed the link between productivity improvements and income growth (*Australian Financial Review* 1995a)?

The answer to this question can only be yes. Past productivity improvements and GDP increases per capita have been due first of all to the substitution of high-quality fossil fuels for the energy of human labour. As these high-quality fuels decline both productivity and income must decline, affecting the material content of the lifestyles of wage earner and stockholder alike (Hall et al., p. ix). Attempts by one to sustain an old lifestyle at the expense of the other are not sustainable. As Bernstein puts it, 'the sight of bulging corporate coffers coexisting with a continuing stagnation in American living standards could become politically untenable' (*Australian Financial Review* 1995b).

It is not enough to know the advantages and disadvantages of potential alternative fuels; we also need to know whether the existing market system will lead to timely decisions to invest in these fuels. As none of these alternatives has an EPR as great as that of oil and gas, the aggregate EPR of the nation's fuel is bound to drop. However, there is a long lag between the expenditure of energy on capital and the flow of energy from the new sources. The authors of *Beyond Oil* modelled this situation for the USA and found if the investment was delayed until fuel quality dropped then *net energy* declined steeply for twenty years before recovery again (Gever et al., pp. 224–5). The decline was much smaller if the critical investments were begun even five years earlier. Remaining high-quality petroleum fuels are needed to commence the change.

USA at the end of the road

The moment of truth is imminent for the USA. As stated earlier the myths underlying the culture do not recognise or accept that natural resources limit the scope for economic and social development. These myths had their genesis in the eighteenth century when the USA had a small population on the eastern seaboard living on the edge of a vast, richly endowed untapped wilderness of seemingly limitless scale. It beckoned hope to millions fleeing Old World misery and intolerance, but bred a free and easy overreaction to the bounty: excessive consumption, the culture of greed, instant gratification and boundless mobility.

The gulf between this obsolete myth and reality is growing rapidly. At some time during the years to 2005 the reality is likely to become too glaring to ignore, precipitating, arguably, the greatest crisis in the USA's 200-year history. The culture of the USA as the hitherto dominant global power pervades all countries. We can expect the consequences to ricochet around the world.

Whether the outcome of this crisis is just, democratic and ecologically sustainable remains to be seen; all three are inextricably linked.

7

Australia: A Fuel's Paradise

The supply and economic quality prospects for oil have been examined at some length; natural gas to a lesser degree. We now need to examine the way oil is used in Australia and our acute dependence on it — at 36 per cent the largest component of *primary energy* use. Primary fuels are those forms of energy obtained directly from nature at the source, as well as renewable fuels such as wood and bagasse, hydro electricity and solar energy. Readers should now realise that Australia's oil self sufficiency is about to decline sharply at a time when acute global supply problems can be expected to emerge. Furthermore, the quality of oil and gas remaining, its economic effectiveness as we have defined it, will decline. Yet governments, mainstream economists, business, transport and urban planners seem blithely unaware of the abyss in front of them. They are driving into the future from the view in the rear-vision mirror.

Energy use patterns

Two thirds of primary energy consumed in Australia is used directly by *end users*, with the remainder consumed by the energy conversion sector, mainly electricity generation from coal. Energy end use is the total energy consumed after the energy conversion sector. It is equal to primary energy less energy consumed or lost in conversion, transmission and distribution. Some primary energy is consumed in oil refineries to convert the crude-oil feedstock to useful refined products.

Petroleum products account for almost half of Australia's energy end use, while transport consumes 37 per cent of all energy end use. Gasoline and diesel comprised 64 per cent and aviation fuels 7 per cent of petroleum product end use in 1993–94. Manufacture of solvents, lubricants, greases, bitumen, waxes, sulphur, explosives, aerosols and feedstocks for plastics and pesticides comprised another 13 per cent of end use (ABARE 1995, p. 53). ABARE does not expect these percentages to change much by 2009–10, except for an end use increase to 12 per cent for aviation. Primary energy consumption is expected to increase from 4174 PJ in 1993–94 to 5506 PJ in 2009–10, a slower increase at 1.7 per cent than occurred in the previous twenty years. The share of natural gas in primary energy consumption is expected to increase from 18 to 23 per cent, mainly for electric power generation and mineral processing in Western Australia.

Figure 7.1 shows ABARE's projected share of total energy consumption for 1993–94, by sector. Mining, commercial and services energy use is expected to grow fastest.

Figure 7.1

PRIMARY ENERGY CONSUMPTION BY SECTOR
1993–94

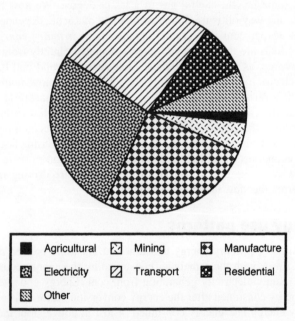

■ Agricultural	⬚ Mining	⬚ Manufacture
⬚ Electricity	⬚ Transport	⬚ Residential
⬚ Other		

Other includes construction, commercial and services

Table 15 in ABARE 1995, p. 33.

This presentation of Australia's energy consumption underestimates the actual total energy used by sectors other than electricity and transport, as the primary energy used by the latter is indirectly consumed by the others. For example, transport costs are 10.4 per cent of agricultural costs, excluding farmers' own use. Road transport accounted for 79 per cent of transport-sector fuel consumption in 1993–94, and is expected to fall to 76 per cent by 2009–10 (ABARE 1995, p. 35).

Our energy efficiency, mainly in manufacturing and transport, has increased by 16.5 per cent over the last twenty years.

In this chapter the broader aspects of petroleum product use in transport are discussed. Chapter 8 will discuss city transport problems. Chapter 9 will discuss energy use in the food system from farm to kitchen and some problems with wheat production. The focus is on road transport and food because of their strategic importance and dependence on petroleum as an energy input.

The structure of transport

Table 7.1 shows how the freight transport task is shared between transport modes. Long-haul carriage of freight tonnage is dominated by shipping and non bulk government rail; interstate road transport is responsible for less than 20 per cent; bulk rail tonnage is dominated by iron ore (private), coal (government), other minerals and grains; and urban freight accounts for most of the intrastate road task.

Table 7.1
Freight task in Australia

Mode	million tonnes	tonne–kilometre (billions)	Average distance (kilometres)
Air	0.15	0.14	930
Sea	43.6	91	2100
Interstate road	15	17	1100
Intrastate road	975	68	70
Bulk rail	285	63	220
Non bulk rail	19	18	950
Total	**1337**	**257**	**190**

Data from Figure 2.2 in Allen Consulting 1993, p. 14. Average distance figures derived from data in columns 1 and 2.

In the twenty years to 1991 the total freight task in tonnes per kilometre has doubled, it has almost quadrupled on urban roads and more than trebled on non urban roads (Austroads 1994, p. 9).

Table 7.2 shows how the passenger transport task is shared between the various modes. Air and non urban bus travel shares have increased significantly since 1971 at the expense of rail and road. Urban car travel has increased at the expense of public transport over the same period and now comprises over 90 per cent of urban vehicle kilometres.

Table 7.2
Passenger transport tasks in Australia (billion passenger–kilometres)

Mode	Urban	Non-urban	Total
Air	—	14	14
Buses	25	18	43
Trams	0.6	—	0.6
Cars	127	49	176
Rail	5.8	1.6	7.4
Total	**158**	**83**	**241**

Data from Figure 2.3 in Allen Consulting 1993, p. 14.

Since 1971 Australia has increased its motor-fuel consumption by 86 per cent and motor vehicle-kilometres by 80 per cent, with trucks and light commercial vehicles leading the way (Austroads 1994, pp. 9, 13). The average load carried by trucks has also increased. We spend 16 per cent of household expenditure on transport, on a par with each of food, housing, and household equipment and operation. Of this transport expenditure, 92 per cent is for private motoring, with fuel comprising 32 per cent of costs (Austroads 1994, p. 6).

Significant reductions in vehicle operating costs since the early 1970s have contributed to these increases in road transport. The life of cars and trucks has increased by 40 per cent while car fuel consumption per kilometre has decreased 50 per cent. Truck fuel consumption has not fallen as much, but trucks have become bigger, faster and more powerful. Car maintenance costs have fallen by as much as 40 per cent, while for articulated trucks they are down to 10 per cent of their 1970 figure (Cox 1994, pp. 30–2). This period has perhaps seen the climax of the motor age, and it is unlikely that further such efficiency gains can be so easily repeated.

Australia has 810 000 kilometres of roads, more per capita than any other country. Only 36 per cent are sealed and another 27 per cent are improved in some way by gravel, crushed stone or other means. We lead the world in road freight per capita. However, 90 per cent of the total road task is carried out on only 20 per cent of the network, mainly in urban areas. Cars account for 87 per cent of our urban passenger-kilometres (Austroads 1994, pp. 1,2,7,14).

Table 7.3 shows the length of our roads in the major classifications as at 1989.

Table 7.3
Australian road classifications 1989

	Urban			Rural	
	Length (km)	Sealed (%)		Length (km)	Sealed (%)
			National H'way	16 100	99
Urban Arterial	15 400	100	Rural Arterial	89 700	81
Urban Local	43 200	91	Rural Local	634 200	19
Total Urban	**58 600**	**94**	**Total Rural**	**734 000**	**28**

Source: Cox 1994, p. 16, selected from Table 2.1.

Eighty-one per cent of traffic is cars and 19 per cent trucks and buses. However, trucks and buses account for 99.9 per cent of pavement loading, which has a major bearing on road life. Two thirds of fuel is used by cars (Austroads 1994, pp. 29, 30).

Roads and the economy

The roads sector of the economy uses about $80 billion per year in resources, some 20 per cent of GDP. Of this, about $43 billion is consumed by the business sector (Cox 1994, p. 3). By comparison domestic rail, sea and air together use only $13.8 billion, and international sea and air transport $17.7 billion (Allen Consulting 1993, p. 13). Table 7.4 breaks down the components of this $80 billion. The vehicle operating costs for cities include an estimated $5 billion for congestion costs, nearly half of which is incurred by business (Cox 1994, p. 26). Urban citizens could rightly consider the cost of air and noise pollution to be higher as this is very much a value judgment.

Historically we have focused on building the rural road network. Those were the days of nation building through construction of communication networks. Political leverage helped shape this priority through the Country Party and its successor, the National Party. The major portion of our rural sealed road network was constructed in the 1950s and 60s, and these roads are now reaching the end of their physical lives. A major outlay on their reconstruction is imminent, and the larger states are those most affected.

Spending on roads during the 1980s matched the growth in traffic, but the proportion spent on capital works declined. The Commonwealth reduced its share of expenditure during the 1990s, arguing that it was only responsible for national highways, and forcing the states to increase their funding (Cox 1994, pp. 41–3). Road expenditure is now some $5.8 billion per year or about 7.5 per cent of the resources consumed by road transport, see Table 7.4.

Table 7.4
Resources consumed by road transport in 1991 (billion dollars)

	Cities	Rural	Total
Private travel — car	13.4	8.7	22.1
Business — car and light commercial vehicles	18.4	10.3	28.7
Truck costs	5.2	7.0	12.2
Bus costs	0.8	0.9	1.7
Accident costs	4.4	3.2	7.6
Air & noise pollution	1.2	0.2	1.3
Road costs	2.2	3.0	5.5
Total	**45.6**	**33.3**	**79.1**

Data aggregated from Tables 4.1 and 4.2 in Cox 1994, pp. 25–6.

These estimates should be treated as broad indicators only. Road user costs exclude taxes. Car business travel includes time.

Business and the road lobby

A cohort of road interests from farmers to motoring organisations, business, local and state governments has come together for road reform. They seek increased federal funding for roads and the refocusing of priorities away from local and rural roads to national highways, urban arterials and freeways — though farmers are lukewarm on the latter. More efficient use of agency road funds are being sought through measures such as the contracting out of work.

The main arguments were first advanced in the 1993 publication *Land Transport Infrastructure*, produced jointly by Allen Consulting Group and the Australian Automobile Association (AAA). The case was developed further by John Cox for the Business Council of Australia (BCA) in *Refocussing Road Reform* (Cox 1994). Their economic arguments underpin the present spate of freeway and privately funded motorways in Brisbane, Sydney, Melbourne and Perth. There has been vigorous public opposition, especially in Sydney and Brisbane.

The impetus behind this reform movement is the competitive pressure on Australian businesses from the rapidly evolving global economy. It is generating a logistics revolution in the manufacturing, service and retail industries. The response of the OECD countries to the

1970s oil crises was to reduce dependence on Middle East oil; strategies were adopted in industry and transport that reduced the economic effectiveness of the fuel base by fuel substitution, and on the other hand improved it by gains in energy efficiency. The other strategy was to transfer manufacturing to undeveloped countries with lower wages, that is, labour that has a lower embodied fossil-fuel content. In the 1990s this trend has extended to service industries such as information technology. The logistics revolution in business is also part of this response.

Materials acquisition, production and distribution of goods now takes place in ever shorter cycle times. This involves smaller production or delivery lots, as parts are only produced when required and not stockpiled as before. Non farm stocks have decreased by about $22 billion since 1980. Transport demand is now being affected by global sourcing, the outsourcing of components from fewer partners on a longer term basis, fewer storage points, and inventories being pushed upstream to suppliers. Niche marketing, production when ordered, just in time processes, flexible and customised distribution are all part of the revolution. Computerised communications facilitate these developments.

Responsiveness to market demands and quick supply arrangements have become as important as cost and quality in this new market environment. Information and transport have substituted for inventory. The quality of transport, its speed, reliability and security, is seen as essential and requires new infrastructure, mostly in outer urban areas where a great many of these new industries and transhipment areas are being established (Cox 1994, pp. 8–11).

Traditional economic justification for roads has been on a local cost-benefit basis for individual projects. Cox argues that the additional larger scale benefits of road projects that enhance the networking of businesses are considerably greater than past project cost-benefit analyses show, hence the push for more urban freeways, arterial roads and national highways. The benefits arise from improving the way businesses can network at lower cost. These freeways, Cox says, should not be built to satisfy commuter demands to the central business districts, but predominantly for business demands in off peak periods. He does not say how to limit peak commuter traffic on these roads other than to use electronic toll charges. Cox argues for Commonwealth funding of these roads as the major economic benefits occur at the total system level, not the local level (Cox 1994, pp. 77–93).

Duplicating two lane highways to four lanes, he says, reduces the number of costly heavy vehicle accidents, and increases capacity fourfold for the additional cost of two lanes, thus encouraging business development along the route and enhancing point to point connectedness at a lower cost. Similar substantial benefits arising from reduced travel time are claimed for freeways that take traffic off traditional stop-start urban arterials, namely:

- a 50–70 per cent reduction in accidents and associated costs;

- a 20–30 per cent reduction in fuel consumption rate;

- a 50–100 per cent reduction in air pollution as engines run at speeds that produce fewer objectionable exhaust emissions;

- a 50 per cent reduction in time for business travel through higher speeds and fewer stops at intersections.

These reductions in accident and emission rates may be real enough, but Cox does not discount these benefits to allow for the enhanced volume of traffic generated by freeways.

The reduction in fuel consumption is offset by the longer distances all vehicles have to travel as a consequence of freeway-generated urban sprawl. Between 1980 and 1983 Newman, Kenworthy and Lyons confirmed this in Perth trials. They found that vehicles in central areas have a 19 per cent lower fuel efficiency than the Perth average due to congestion, but that central-area residents used 22 per cent less fuel. Conversely, congestion-free outer suburban driving is 12 per cent more fuel efficient than average but residents use 29 per cent more fuel. They found a similar relationship for exhaust emissions. Similar relationships held for thirty-two other cities around the world (Newman, Kenworthy & Lyons 1988). Urban sprawl increases both total fuel consumption, the cost that ultimately counts, and another important business cost, travel time over longer distances, also confirmed by Newman et al. Further statistics illustrate the point for Australian cities. From 1961 to 1981:

- population density fell from 19 to 14 people per hectare;

- car ownership rose from 221 to 453 per thousand people;

- petrol use per capita rose from 17 100 to 29 800 MJ per year.

These trends have continued. Between 1976 and 1988 car travel per person has increased 22 per cent in Adelaide, 30 per cent in Perth and Sydney, 47 per cent in Melbourne and 51 per cent in Brisbane (Newman & Kenworthy 1991).

Cox says fuel and time savings for business and the public are large in comparison to the funds spent on roads. But the reverse is almost certainly the case because of these offsetting distance factors. Nor does he allow for the higher cost of other services arising from urban sprawl such as water and waste water, pollution of rivers and estuaries like the Hawkesbury River west of Sydney, and sheer consumption of the landscape and scarce well-watered fertile farmland.

These indirect costs quickly become a business cost and depress the incomes of most households, thus shrinking markets.

Allen Consulting modelled for the AAA the impacts of investment in infrastructure on productivity growth and gains in other economy-wide outcomes such as GDP. They used a modified long run version of the Industry Commission's MR-ORANI general equilibrium model of the economy. Their version of the model uses economic benefits distributed to various industry sectors as assessed from several road investment case studies based on the cost-benefit approach. The model is constructed around an input-output database for the Australian economy. This provides a detailed numerical picture of the inputs and cost structure of the economy and the sales disposition of the outputs produced. Economic behaviour is imposed via mathematical equations describing how the underlying input-output structures of the economy change with relative movements in prices of output and factors of production, productivity shifts, taste changes and shifts in trading conditions in the international markets. ORANI is based on the neoclassical economic model of market behaviour.

The effect of a 1990–91 $1 billion investment in each of urban freeways, arterial and local roads, and rural national, arterial and local roads was studied. Investment benefits were evaluated over the estimated thirty-five-year physical life of the roads and will take several years to become manifest. The modelling found that these investments gave an annual percentage increase in GDP after ten years of 0.2 for urban arterial roads, 0.15 for urban freeways, 0.07 for rural national and arterial roads, and 0.03 for rural and urban local roads (Allen Consulting 1993, pp. 57–76). These benefits claimed for the first three road classes were much higher than those obtained from local cost-benefit studies. They are a consequence of benefits arising from enhanced networking at the national and regional scale. Hence the push to reallocate funds to urban freeways and arterial roads.

There are a thousand assumptions built into this model, requiring value judgments by the modeller. The model outcome is very much a product of these judgments. Many of the assumptions bear little relationship to the real world. Here are some cited by Cox, together with comments:

- 'Wage rates adjust to clear labour markets.' This infers wages go up and down freely with employment levels, without significant resistance or action by the work force. It also implies workers easily move around the country from job to job at no cost.

- 'Industry and economy wide stocks of capital adjust to maintain given rates of return.' This means that under-utilised or under-performing capital is swiftly shifted to new profitable investment, like labour. Frictionless change without significant elapsed time.

- 'Tax rates adjust to uniformly maintain a real public sector borrowing requirement.' Governments can do this without much difficulty, and in any case do adjust tax rates to this end.

- 'Nominal household savings are a fixed proportion of nominal household consumption.' We all dutifully do this!

- 'Real investment is a fixed proportion of the real capital stock.' It never is.

Brian Toohey in his book *Tumbling Dice* describes the history of neoclassical economic theory on which ORANI is based. Chapter 9 describes in considerable detail the history and assumptions underlying the ORANI model (Toohey 1994, p. 175). He lists some for short run applications as:

- Perfect competition with all product markets clearing so that prices equal marginal costs. (There are no monopolies or price makers. ORANI cannot deal with market power, transaction costs, information issues, the role of skills, innovation or managerial efficiency.)

- No stock holdings by companies, so output always equals sales. (Stocks are on trucks on roads! Instantaneous sales.)

- No financial sector. (It is so efficient it consumes no resources and implies instant transactions!)

- Labour is homogeneous, fully mobile and fully utilised. (ORANI modelling starts and ends with full employment! There are no impediments to this mobility.)

- Capital is fully utilised. (Rarely, if ever, does business make perfect decisions.)

- No balance of payments constraint. (We wait with bated breath every month!)

- No impact on interest rates from either budget or current account deficits. (Ditto!)

- The nominal exchange rate is fixed. (It is?)

- Demand for commodity exports is highly responsive to small price changes. (Highly exaggerated!)

ORANI betrays its neoclassical thinking through a lack of appreciation of duration.

Toohey says some of the most trenchant critics of ORANI are former Industry Commission employees. Bodies like the Industry Commission give policy advice to governments and others based on modelling of this kind, and Toohey says the commission is the most extensive user of the ORANI model. That advice to a considerable degree aims to mould the real world to fit the assumptions of the model. These economists always speak of imperfect markets, but rarely of imperfect theories.

Lubulwa pointed out that equations used to describe the demand for transport in ORANI in 1985 were ad hoc as they were not based on optimising behaviour. The modeller has to make the choices! Furthermore, ORANI does not attempt to model passenger transport (Lubulwa 1986).

Can anyone seriously believe the economic benefits attributed to freeways and arterial highways by Allen Consulting and Cox when these are based on such dubious assumptions? And there are many more. But the biggest and most damaging of all their assumptions concerns fuel supplies for the next thirty-five years. Neither book mentions, let alone discusses, fuel availability, affordability or quality as a measure of economic effectiveness. For organisations like the AAA and BCA this is inexcusable.

Cox claims that the large-scale effects of infrastructure investments as revealed by macro-econometric analyses like MR-ORANI depend on the scale of the variables being examined, the effects are greatest at a national level, and least at the local level. The more aggregated studies capture the indirect benefits at the total economy level. He says these gains arise from the *law of comparative advantage* of different economic regions coming into play — transport allows regions with different resources to grow by specialisation to the mutual benefit of both through trade (Cox 1994, p. 91). Similar arguments are used to justify free trade, as embodied in the rules of the new World Trade Organisation (WTO) that is replacing the General Agreement on Tariffs and Trade (GATT).

David Ricardo first expounded the so called law of comparative advantage early in the nineteenth century. He was a pioneer in economic theory and advocate of free trade. However, there is one often overlooked vital condition necessary for the mutual benefits of free trade to occur. Neither capital nor labour should be mobile across national boundaries. These have never been more mobile than today. Capital flows around the world electronically in seconds at a volume greatly exceeding that of traded goods. Daly and Cobb in *For The Common Good* elaborate on this theme at length (Daly & Cobb 1989, pp. 209–35).

Do Cox and Allen Consulting imply that capital and labour should not be mobile between nations and regions within Australia? That international money markets should be regulated out of existence? What does the real situation mean for regional Australia and many nations? Most likely inside Australia a further decline and decay of rural and regional communities with major urban regions becoming megacities existing in increasingly stressed, overloaded and unsustainable environments. Internationally, a shift of industries to countries with the lowest wages, worst working conditions and minimal environmental safeguards (Daly 1993).

This is not to deny validity to the law of comparative advantage within the right environmental and transport constraints. Prime consideration must be given to the environmental and resource constraints that together limit the scale and scope of economic activity. It is these constraints that Cox and Allen Consulting ignore — entirely in the case of fuel for vehicles. The scale of the economy, its size, is important (Daly 1993).

There cannot be a global economy without abundant cheap transport, without an abundant supply of affordable fuel — petroleum.

Roads generate traffic

In his book *Parkinson's Law*, Northcote Parkinson satirised management and bureaucracy. One of his 'laws' was: 'work expands according to the number of people available to do it'. Anti-freeway activists have always maintained that traffic expands to saturate the roads built for it, a view generally played down by the pro-freeway lobby. They now have vindication for their belief.

In 1994 the UK Department of Transport published a report, *Trunk Roads and the Generation of Traffic*, prepared by the Standing Advisory Committee on Trunk Road Assessment (SACTRA 1994). In 1979 British prime minister Margaret Thatcher had initiated what she called 'the great car economy' (*Australian Financial Review* 1994g). Road building gathered pace during the 1980s. Then road funding was increased by 70 per cent in the five years to 1993 (Cox 1994, p. 57). A massive protest movement has arisen involving hundreds of anti-motorway lobby groups from all sectors of society. They brought about a change in British thinking: the future must have less car use, not more! The revolt against the car has been a major reason for the collapse in support for John Major's Conservative government. The vision of the great car economy has ended and the SACTRA report was a response to this vast movement.

The report convincingly shows that major road works in the UK generate or 'induce' traffic beyond the level predicted by the designers — for London's M25 orbital road perhaps by as much as 40 per cent (SACTRA 1994; *New Scientist* 1995). SACTRA found that the amount of travel undertaken by vehicle users depends on petrol prices and reductions in travel time in particular. Roads can induce land development that soon generates more traffic. The report concluded that induced traffic can and does occur, probably quite extensively, though its size and significance are likely to vary in different circumstances.

Studies reviewed by SACTRA demonstrated convincingly that the economic value of a scheme can be overestimated by the omission of even a small amount of induced traffic. They showed in particular that traffic increases on improved roads are, in general, not offset by equivalent reductions on unimproved alternative routes.

The report said induced traffic is of greatest importance where:

- the network is operating or is expected to operate close to capacity;

- traveller responsiveness to changes in travel times or costs is high, as may occur where trips are suppressed by congestion and then released when the network is improved;

- the implementation of a scheme causes large changes in travel costs.

This is most likely to occur around urban areas, estuary crossings, and strategic capacity enhancing interurban schemes, including motorway widening. These effects can occur some distance away from the road. SACTRA said that regional strategic appraisal needs strengthening by the following:

- Decisions on schemes in one part of a corridor should not precommit environmentally sensitive decisions elsewhere without thorough economic and environmental appraisal of the overall strategy.

- The consequences for the pattern of land use and development need to be considered at a regional level.

- Since traffic is stimulated in part by network quality, induced traffic effects must be considered at the wider network level, that is, city-wide or even wider.

Faced with this popular revolt the British government has seen the light and since mid-1994 has: scrapped 270 motorway proposals worth 19 billion pounds sterling; cut 1.16 billion pounds sterling (one third) from the road budget; increased funding for public transport; prevented all new edge of city shopping centres; and established powerful planning guidelines to minimise the need for travel within cities (*Daily Telegraph* 1995).

They began to recognise that investment in public transport is twice as effective as road building in the economy, that car use is very costly when all costs are considered, and that investment is not attracted to smog-filled, traffic-dominated cities. When announcing the one third reduction in road building, the British Transport Minister said:

A deteriorating environment in the form of worsening air quality, degraded towns and cities, and damaged landscapes would make the United Kingdom an unattractive place for investors and would cost a great deal in economic terms as well as in our physical health and the quality of our lives. (*Daily Telegraph* 1995)

Another major reason to urgently shift away from a car economy is that cars need petroleum fuel. A reason bigger than all the others put together.

Induced traffic will further reduce the economic benefits attributed to urban road works by Cox and Allen Consulting, especially as these appear to be sensitive to even small levels of induced traffic. Australian state capital cities, Sydney and Melbourne in particular, are the ones most likely to experience induced traffic.

8
Chaotic Cities

Australia's state capital cities have chronic traffic problems, most acute in Sydney, Melbourne and Brisbane. Politicians and road agencies seem to think the solution is more roads, reinforced by the arguments of Cox and Allen Consulting. These have been given the blessing of the Business Council of Australia in the name of international competitiveness.

Road capital stocks have declined 50 per cent since 1975 according to Cox (Cox 1994, p. 128). By contrast, he says capital stocks of private and public trading enterprises have kept pace with GDP. This is another argument he uses for increased urban and national highway expenditure for the benefit of business. Spend more on roads and, ipso facto, GDP grows. This is going down Margaret Thatcher's UK cul-de-sac.

Urban road advocates have a cavalier attitude to the consequences for our cities when they stubbornly push more roads on to an increasingly hostile and resentful population. Governments now lose office over these issues.

Sydney

Sydney has the most congested urban roads in Australia and Perth the least, well illustrated in Table 8.1.

Funding constraints and Loan Council borrowing limits in the 1980s led the New South Wales government to enter into complex financing and contract arrangements with three companies to build privately owned and operated roads for Sydney. These were the Sydney Harbour Tunnel (SHT) linking the Central Business District (CBD) with North Sydney, the M4 Motorway paralleling Parramatta Road in the western suburbs, and part of the M5 Motorway in the south-western suburbs. All opened for traffic in 1992.

Table 8.1
Urban arterial road statistics, early 1980s

	Sydney	Melb.	Bris.	Adel.	Perth	Total
Population (000s)	2956	2340	971	910	846	8024
Daily travel (mill. vehicle km per day)	31.1	32.5	11.8	11.4	14.8	101.6
Cars (000s)	1204	1213	463	424	444	3748
Road space (lane/km)	3450	6369	2348	2268	3033	17468
Ave. number of lanes	2.3	3.6	2.3	3.4	2.9	3.1
Ave. daily traffic (veh/day/arterial)	21500	18200	16500	16900	13900	17800
Lane-km/1000 cars	**2.9**	**5.3**	**5.1**	**5.3**	**6.8**	**4.7**
Lane-km/1000 people	**1.2**	**2.7**	**2.4**	**2.5**	**3.5**	**2.2**

Source: Maunsell 1992, p. 33, table 6.2.

They were the subject of a special audit by the New South Wales Auditor-General in 1994 at the direction of Parliament. He found that post-construction financial risks for the SHT rested almost entirely with the Roads and Traffic Authority (RTA) through a complex range of commitments and guarantees made with the SHT company. If it could be held that the private sector was the principal, then no Loan Council approvals would have been required, and the financial risks would not be seen as public sector obligations. A form of off-balance-sheet financing. He said these potential RTA liabilities could become several times the $560 million construction cost. He therefore considered the RTA had effective ownership of the tunnel, claims hotly disputed by the RTA (Auditor-General 1994).

Within two years the SHT had 'induced' an extra 30 000 vehicles to cross the harbour, creating a crisis that left city residents and local councils outraged. Small accidents bring disaster to the inner city for hours. Gridlock! The streets are more hostile, dirty and dangerous; there is more air pollution; communities are more deeply divided by rivers of concrete. The $170 million Glebe Island Bridge shifts the gridlock somewhere else.

The Auditor-General says the financial risks for the M4 and M5 motorways are more equitably shared between the RTA and the two companies, Statewide Roads for the M4 and Interlink Roads Pty Ltd for the M5. He also raised other questions of propriety surrounding the association of an ex-premier and former executives of the RTA with Statewide Roads or companies associated with Statewide Roads and the SHT (Auditor-General 1994, p. 93).

Within months total traffic increased 33 per cent on Parramatta Road and the M4 after the latter's opening (*Parramatta Advertiser* 1994). A clear case of induced traffic, and illustrating the extreme vulnerability of Sydney to this phenomenon.

Not to be deterred, the New South Wales Fahey government late in 1994 approved another privately funded 20 kilometre motorway, the M2 between the Lane Cove River and Baulkham Hills. Construction has begun, but only after vigorous protests, with people chaining themselves to bulldozers, and nearly 100 arrests.

The total cost will be $655 million with the company, Hills Motorway Pty Ltd, providing $485 million, and the government $50 million for various overpasses and $120 million to buy the land which will be leased to the company. Several superannuation funds are providing $155 million of equity, banks $100 million and institutional investors $200 million of CPI-linked bonds with twenty-seven years minimum to maturity. A stock exchange float of $1.3 million was involved. There is a thirty-six-year concession period with options to extend to 45 years (*Australian Financial Review* 1994d). The company forecasts returns of 10 per cent before soaring to 40–50 per cent towards the end of the thirty-six to forty-five-year concession period (*Australian Financial Review* 1994e).

Bob Walker, professor of accounting at the University of New South Wales, probing information related to the prospectus for the stock issue, found that Hills Motorway Ltd expects $408.6 million in financial support from the state government. This takes the form of promissory notes for deferred payment of rent on the motorway land, these to be issued between 1998 and 2025. Repayments are budgeted to be made between 2028 and 2042 when principal and interest are expected to be some $546 million! He says taxpayers face a considerable risk, despite the then Transport Minister, Bruce Baird, telling Parliament that 'all the risk' would be borne by the private sector (Walker 1994). The risk is even bigger when future fuel supply scenarios are ignored. And this is not all! The RTA can be liable for compensation to Hills Motorway under a wide range of ill-defined scenarios, where these can be demonstrated to detract from the expected return on investment. These include:

- upgrading of Epping Road or other roads in the region that might take traffic from the M2;

- introducing public transport initiatives that have 'a material adverse impact';

- extension of the motorway;

- certain adverse legislation or judicial proceedings.

This penalises significant government public transport initiatives for up to forty-five years.

The world will consume 1000 billion barrels of oil in that time, equal to present world reserves or one third more than has already been consumed. These forecast returns are sheer fantasy. But this is still not all!

The prospectus says the RTA has undertaken to manage the Sydney metropolitan traffic system so as to 'recognise the position of the M2 as the principal arterial road servicing specified regions of north western Sydney' (Hills Motorway 1994). This includes reference to 'timely maintenance, the importance of other roads' and 'ensuring the free flow of traffic'. The cost of these RTA road works conceivably linked to the M2 to a greater or lesser degree could be up to $1000 million. Certainly the RTA's road program for decades over a large area of Sydney will have to pivot around the need to maintain the profitability of the M2. Such limitations will be devastating to good town planning.

The prospectus contains a Traffic Assessment Report. It forecasts daily toll traffic rising from 78 287 in 1998 to 106 650 in 2027, with the greatest increases in the earlier years. The impact of future fuel availability and economics on these forecasts is not discussed. The prospectus also says that:

> Subject to the terms of the Project Documents, the Company and the Trustee accept all the risks of the Project, including the costs of the Project and the risks that revenue and traffic volume may be less than estimated. (Hills Motorway 1994)

This suggests that New South Wales taxpayers are not responsible for losses due to low traffic levels arising from the future petroleum supply scenarios discussed in earlier chapters. The scope for litigation and dispute around these issues is thus enormous.

A major social and economic catastrophe is in the making for Sydney, and indeed Australia, given our understanding of the emerging petroleum supply situation over the next twenty years, let alone the next forty.

These issues surrounding motorways were a prime factor leading to the defeat of the Fahey government in April 1995, and the return of a Labor government under Bob Carr.

Brisbane

South East Queensland is Australia's most livable region. The environment, the public and private facilities, the amenities and the general quality of life are second to none in the nation. This unique lifestyle must be preserved and protected.

That is how a Queensland government discussion paper on transport strategies for South East Queensland begins (Queensland Government 1995). Of course, the citizens of Adelaide, Melbourne, Sydney and Perth say the same thing about their cities.

Under the heading 'Consider these trends — is this what you want?', the discussion paper says that South East Queensland's (SEQ) population is expected to grow by 60 per cent or 1 million by 2011, with an 80 per cent increase in transport trips to 10.5 million per day. Public transport would remain at its present level of 8 per cent of trips. The number of road vehicles is expected to increase by about 500 000. Furthermore, the report says SEQ is particularly prone to pollution problems because of its climate and geography. Motor vehicles are already responsible for an estimated 45 per cent of air pollution and 34 per cent of greenhouse gas emissions. Chronic respiratory illnesses such as asthma, bronchitis and emphysema, as well as minor eye, nose and throat irritations, can be expected to increase. Social and environmental degradation will also increase. State government studies say Brisbane faces a Los Angeles-type smog problem because of its climate and topography (*Courier-Mail* 1994).

Queensland is Australia's fastest growing state, especially in the south-east and around Cairns. The SEQ population has been increasing at the rate of 1000 per week in the 1990s. Understandably, acute pressures have arisen on service and infrastructure provision. The discussion paper says SEQ transport has a budget of $1 billion in 1994–95, half of it for roads. A substantial increase would be needed by 2011 to support the car habit. Several hundred million dollars are being spent on an electric commuter railway from the Gold Coast to Brisbane.

Most of the discussion paper outlines concepts that could achieve a better fit between transport and urban planning to contain urban sprawl — which means limiting the role of the motor car and favouring public transport. It says the vast majority of freight movements are over short distances and to highly dispersed destinations. The transport planners are faced with a dynamic situation threatening to run away from them.

The discussion paper concludes:

Meeting the increasingly difficult transport task will require a shift away from previous policies and planning assumptions which were biased in favour of cars. At the same time, there will be a need to avoid unnecessarily penalising motorists as they go about earning incomes and enjoying life.

Nowhere in the discussion paper is the question of future fuel supplies for transport even mentioned as an issue.

From the tone of the discussion paper everything seems fine on the SEQ urban and transport development front. Nothing could be further from the truth. More than any of Australia's cities, Brisbane and its hinterland has lacked a metropolitan-wide regional plan, a legacy left by a National Party government not inclined to such initiatives. The pace of development has outstripped the capacity of the government to develop strategic land-use and infrastructure plans. There are poorly coordinated efforts; SEQ2001, a SEQ land-use report, was published in 1994 followed by an Integrated Regional Transport Plan Phase 1 report early in 1995. Preparation of Phase 2 commenced in the winter of 1995. Land-use and transport plans should be integrated.

Transport infrastructure in SEQ has given the Queensland government its greatest headache. There has been fierce opposition to road projects, with numerous protest meetings attended by thousands. The most contentious was the $500–700 million South Coast Motorway from Brisbane to the Logan River, halfway to the Gold Coast. A privately funded tollway was proposed. It was intended to relieve traffic on the Pacific Highway, where passenger trips increased 23 per cent in 1994. It was to join the South East freeway, the major southern gateway to central Brisbane, where traffic is banked up for several kilometres at peak hours. The tollway proposal generated the strongest protests because of the disruptive impact it would have on the environment, koala sanctuaries, state forests, and social amenity (*Bulletin* 1994).

The critics say a new road would not solve the traffic problem. Pacific Highway would still be crowded by motorists trying to avoid tolls on the new road. And the new road would quickly become congested if the expected population growth occurs — requiring yet another road (*Courier-Mail* 1995). Another proposed toll road to Brisbane Airport which would slice through the city's inner northern suburbs has attracted strong protests as well, including from Brisbane's Lord Mayor, Jim Soorley. He argues for greater public transport funding (*Courier-Mail* 1995a). But the realism of his proposal for dedicated busways is questioned by others.

Queensland Premier Wayne Goss promised during the July 1995 state election campaign to link Brisbane's CBD and airport by rail, double the use of public transport and create a new Transit Authority for SEQ. There is a widely held belief that Brisbane is set to undergo a traffic and public transport revolution (*Courier-Mail* 1995b).

The Queensland Transport Department has responded to this flak by retreating to its bunker. The lobby group New Ways Not Freeways (NWNF) says that in recent transport legislation the Department has relieved itself of the obligation to consult or even to be subject to judicial review (NWNF 1995). The Goss government has been retreating on plans for early public involvement in planning for the next freeway and narrowed the terms of reference to consultants assessing the Inner City Bypass to avoid examining alternatives (*Australian* 1994b).

This furore over motorways cost the Goss Labor government four SEQ seats in the July 1995 elections. An end is needed to ad hoc government road proposals that undermine its own policy processes for an integrated SEQ land and transport strategy, according to Mark Finnane, an anti-freeway activist (*Courier-Mail* 1995c). There are some small signs of change, the South Coast Motorway was abandoned in September 1995 in favour of widening Pacific Highway to six lanes over four years at a cost of $200 million (*Courier-Mail* 1995d). But that decision only focuses ever more sharply; what is the long-term transport strategy. Perhaps if the Goss government recognised the need to think beyond oil its transport planning problems would become much easier.

Melbourne

Melbourne has more freeways and arterial roads than any other city in Australia (see Table 8.1). It also has the world's largest urban rail system in relation to population and the largest tram system outside Europe. Patronage on these transit systems has declined; they are under-utilised, service standards and management are poor, and annual deficits are high (PTUA 1995). Some rail cars and trams are in mothballs. Yet peak-hour traffic on roads to the inner city crawls in queues up to 10 kilometres long.

Jeff Kennett's government revived the ambitious freeway program of twenty-five years ago when elected in 1992. The program's main elements had been cancelled in the 1970s after vigorous public objections. The new program would add 211 kilometres of freeway to an existing 150 kilometres at a cost that could reach A$6500 million. It is now the largest urban freeway extension program in the developed world (PTUA 1995).

The first of these new freeways is the 22 kilometre City Link project around the CBD and joining the Tullamarine freeway at Flemington with the South East Arterial Road at Kooyong. It will cost $1700 million, be six to eight lanes wide, and is to be financed, constructed and operated as a tollway by a private company. Widening of part of the Tullamarine freeway to eight lanes and part of the South

East Arterial Road to six lanes is included. The road will have two crossings of the Yarra River, one by bridge, the other by tunnel and an extensive elevated section crossing roads and railways near Footscray. Jeff Kennett has described it as the biggest public infrastructure project since the Snowy Mountains Scheme. Three hundred thousand vehicles per day are expected to use it. Tolls will be collected for thirty-four years, and transfer to public ownership will occur in 2033 (*Age* 1995b).

Jeff Kennett defended the project as environmentally sound because 'it is going to take so much of our traffic off suburban streets and smaller roads. It is also going to bring about a quicker flow of traffic, so the traffic does not idle, sit at lights and bottleneck' (*Age* 1995). However, Vicroads' own published figures show that twelve important roads allegedly 'relieved' by City Link will actually be carrying substantially more traffic after it opens (Vicroads 1994). And this is before the effects of 'induced' traffic come into play, as discussed earlier. City Link is located where SACTRA says this factor has the greatest impact. Should a small minority of rail passengers shift to cars City Link's claimed benefits will be cancelled out. Road engineers must be the only business people who think that improving their product won't get more customers!

The government has confirmed that Transurban, a joint venture between a Japanese company, Obayashi, and Transfield Holdings, has the go ahead for the project. Transurban is going to raise funds from industry superannuation funds, private and institutional investors, and by a $500 million equity issue on the stock exchange late in 1995 or early 1996. The details will be revealed in the prospectus (*Australian* 1995c). The government is providing $88 million in the form of land and $159 million for 'necessary state works', including environmental, recreational and road works in adjacent areas. The *Age* newspaper believes repayment of the $247 million to the government is likely about 2013 after Transurban has paid project debts. Any super profits would be shared with the government, and earnings are expected to be about $200 million in the first year. The state government has not underwritten the project, but has guaranteed to oversee its refinancing if Transurban does not fulfil its commitments (*Age* 1995c).

Tolls on the City Link will range from 80 cents to $3 for cars over six toll zones. Transponders provided by Transurban and attached to vehicles will activate sensors at tollgates and record tollway travel on a computer. Motorists will either be sent bills or can have credit accounts. Vehicles will not stop at the tollgates (*Age* 1995b), but motorists evading tolls would be photographed and fined by the government. The Opposition leader claims the government would introduce tolls on other roads once the transponders were fitted to cars (*Age* 1995a).

But Cox sees this going much further: automated highway systems. Vehicles will travel along roads not controlled by the driver but by the road itself. The vehicle will drive itself by computer on an automated track. Driver error will be eliminated, and sensors will link road and vehicle to maximise vehicle performance and road traffic capacity. An unattainable level of technical performance and reliability would be required, totally immune to human tinkering. Cox is quite serious about this and sees the following advantages accruing (Cox 1994, p. 35):

- higher traffic capacity, as measured by vehicles per lane per hour;

- significantly better driving safety as human error is eliminated, particularly under adverse weather conditions;

- enhanced mobility for disabled, old and inexperienced drivers;

- reduced fuel consumption and pollutant emissions because of constant speeds;

- increased reliability of travel times for public transport and commercial vehicles involved in just in time deliveries;

- better use of land space.

Think of the sheer terror of travelling bumper to bumper at 100 km/hour!

Most Melburnians do not want tolls, according to opinion polls. Election analyst Malcolm Mackerras predicts tolls will cost the Kennett government two thirds of its majority at the next election. Jeff Kennett, of course, rejected this claim (*Australian* 1995a).

None of the City Link documents and media reports mention the issue of future fuel supplies for vehicles. Melbourne more than any other Australian city can swiftly and inexpensively make a significant shift to a less car-based urban form. It has extensive under-utilised public transport capacity. Large-scale investment is not needed. Already twenty of the major shopping centres are located at railway stations (PTUA 1995). There is even a comprehensive report on how this might be done. *Moving Melbourne* was produced in 1991 by the nine inner-city councils belonging to the Inner Metropolitan Regional Association Inc (IMRA 1991). They were concerned about the declining population and employment base of the region, under-utilised infrastructure, environmental degradation, traffic congestion, and decline of public transport. The report examined transport and land-use issues in an integrated way using a public consultation process.

Moving Melbourne stresses that public transport is not an end in itself but a means to achieving a wide range of important objectives, namely to:

- make the region more livable and to increase its human vitality;

- permit and encourage population and employment intensification;

- help enhance the region's economic role and performance;

- assist in reducing pollution and other environmental impacts;

- reduce congestion and other direct traffic impacts such as poor road safety;

- improve convenience and ease of accessibility to all urban activities for all people;

- conserve energy in transport;

- assist movement of freight required to be carried by road.

The report proposes ten principles and key initiatives to achieve these objectives together with specific recommendations for revitalising inner Melbourne public transport over ten years. The major thrust was towards improving service delivery: more frequent services, upgrading of stations, tram and bus stops to be attractive, safer and more friendly places. Better integration of rail, tram and bus timetables was proposed to make mode change easy, with priority for transit. There was a focus on passenger information, marketing and education initiatives. Land-use planning was linked with public transport. Concurrent measures to discourage car commuter traffic were included. A small number of rail and tram extensions were proposed, mainly to enhance system interconnections. A substantial shift of passengers from cars to public transport, bicycles and walking over ten years was possible. The consequent reduced traffic and congestion would improve the roads for commercial traffic, a particular concern of John Cox. Better use would be made of all existing urban infrastructure. Initiatives like these would achieve the transport benefits for business that Cox is seeking.

The *Moving Melbourne* project was based on an extensive consultation process with a wide range of organisations, professional bodies, transport agencies and community interests — anyone who had a stake in the inner city's future. Problems and issues were first identified in workshops from which solutions emerged over a wide front. This is the only way to approach the complex issues surrounding urban transport and land use.

It would not be difficult to extend these measures to the rest of Melbourne. Perhaps as Melburnians realise the full implications of City Link their opposition will become strong enough to end what must be the most disastrous infrastructure investment ever proposed for their city.

Perth

Western Australia has the lion's share of national highways and an extensive rural and remote area road system. Perth has more roads per person than any other state capital and they sprawl over the landscape more than in any other city. In the 1990s SEQ has overtaken Perth as the fastest growing metropolitan region.

Western Australia faces four road transport problems. First, Pilbara mineral and petroleum development creates demands for roads over long distances for heavy freight traffic. Second, the Eyre Highway across the Nullarbor Plain carries growing freight traffic and needs substantial upgrading and widening to avoid pavement failures. There also happens to be a recently upgraded railway paralleling the highway. Third, the rural network from Geraldton to Esperance is reaching the end of its life and expensive rebuilding is needed by 2005. Finally, Perth has reached a stage where ever more expensive road works are now needed to cope with continued car dependency, the highest in Australia.

In 1994 the Commissioner of Main Roads, Ken Michael, said the average age of sealed roads was increasing. Some $2 billion was needed over the next ten years for their preservation alone. He said present funding provided only 30 per cent of this with additional funds required for new works as well (Michael 1994). He said sealed rural roads have a life of forty years. Ageing roads are a growing problem in other states as well, though more so in the west due to the state's size.

A cohort of road transport interests, from the Main Roads Department to trucking associations, together with rural interests, local government and the Royal Automobile Club, set up in 1994 a lobby group called Fix Australia Fix The Roads (FAFTR). Their central objective is to increase Federal funding for roads based mainly on the economic rationale and priorities of Cox and Allen Consulting. The campaign has since become national, but under different banners in other states. A central role is played by the Road Transport Forum, the peak body of the road transport industry.

Questioned at their FAFTR Summit in April 1994 about the fact that their campaign did not consider future fuel supplies as the key strategic issue, the speakers' responses indicated their thinking.

Stuart Hicks, Director-General of Transport, said Australia needed a balance between all forms of transport. Eric Charlton, National Party Minister for Transport, said 'Australia could not be isolated from the world scene ... For us to change our economy in isolation ... would be economic suicide'. He then went on to say: 'but as one fuel runs down something will take its place ...' This is the typical answer to this question. Have faith, technology will come to the rescue. John Cox said that 'Even with increased demand we would not have an increase in fuel consumption because there could be technological solutions which would reduce fuel consumption by even more than current trends — for instance hydrogen and electric powered transport ... thus avoiding the question, yet we have already discussed how cars increase city fuel consumption, and in chapter 5 the prospects for hydrogen and electric-powered transport. Howard Croxon, President of WA Road Transport, could only say, that 'we have to export, we have to cart ...' (FAFTR1994).

To ignore the economic consequences of future fuel supply options for road investments that will last to the middle of the twenty-first century is the ultimate in political and economic irresponsibility. These lobbyists do themselves, their constituency and the community a grave disservice.

Needless to say, the Federal government did not respond with extra road funds. So in April 1995 the Western Australian Court government imposed a state-wide 4 cents per litre levy on petrol sales to raise some $700 million for roads over ten years. This was after diverting other funds to roads following their election in 1993.

The first five years of this levy will go to build the Northern City Bypass. This is a 7.5 kilometre six lane highway along the northern boundary of the CBD, linking the main north-south freeway with the Great Eastern Highway in the city's eastern suburbs. Construction is planned from mid-1996 to 2000. It has been on Perth's regional plan since 1963. The road has been fiercely opposed by inner-city residents and businesses for fifteen years. Their resistance has forced the government to put 1.6 kilometres in a tunnel at an additional cost of some $80 million pushing the total to some $370 million, including related works. Rural motorists will be wondering why they should be paying one third of the cost via the levy. It can only succeed in 'inducing' extra traffic into the inner city as already discussed.

Perth's suburban railway was electrified during the 1990s and a new northern suburbs line built down the middle of the Mitchell Freeway, 29 kilometres to Joondalup. Buses were integrated with rail. There has been a dramatic increase in passengers, reversing a long decline in public transport patronage. However, the Northern City Highway proposal presented for public comment in 1993 did not have an alternative to build on this initiative and diminish the role of the motor car and dependence on petroleum. It is not known whether the Northern City Bypass is the best way to spend nearly 400 million dollars! Neither FAFTR, the Northern City Highway documents nor Perth's regional plan, Metroplan, address the important strategic issue of future fuel supplies.

Shifting to a less car-orientated focus in Perth is not easy; due to the extreme degree of urban sprawl it is difficult to introduce attractive economical alternatives like public transport. But this is all the more reason to change now, not reinforce the present pattern as the Northern City Highway will do.

Adelaide

Adelaide's population growth is the lowest of any state capital. It lacks the extreme traffic stresses and congestion problems of other cities. The large area of parkland around the CBD has significantly reduced the scope for inner-city congestion. However, Adelaide is Australia's economically weakest mainland city, the one perhaps most vulnerable to the economic consequences of the coming decline of oil. Adelaide is not deeply enmeshed in the freeway craze. Perhaps there are advantages in being a small city with low growth.

There are two projects that echo events in other cities. One is Crafers Highway on the road to Melbourne where it climbs over the Adelaide Hills. The other is the 22 kilometre Southern Expressway from Darlington to the Onkaparinga River.

The $136 million six lane Crafers Highway will replace a 10 kilometre four lane winding road on the Mt Lofty Ranges escarpment. The existing road has a high accident rate and traffic is expected to increase 29 per cent by 2006. This road has more justification than those discussed in other cities, given its location and accident rate. However, a case could be made for keeping it at four lanes, especially as the Melbourne-Adelaide railway has just been converted to dual standard-broad gauge. All southern state capitals are now connected by standard-gauge rail. Rail freight transport is more energy efficient than road transport, especially on long hauls.

The $112 million first-stage Southern Expressway is proposed as a single two lane carriageway to function as a one way road northwards in the morning peak and as a sole south-bound road during the evening peak. The second stage will add another two lanes, when it will become a normal two way road. It caters to urban sprawl and will reinforce social isolation and alienation in these distant southern suburbs. The growing number of people without access to a car will find it even more difficult to get around. Public transport alternatives have not been considered.

Adelaide has a diesel-powered passenger rail system centred on the CBD. Electrification, together with integration of buses with this rail system, and attention to service standards as in Perth, could help turn the tide towards public transport. The cost would be similar to the $250 million for Perth's electrification. There is scope in Adelaide for redevelopment along the railways, especially on the northern line to Elizabeth. The shift away from petroleum-dependent transport would need to be a major justification. But a revisioning of Adelaide is needed before this can happen.

Wouldn't it be nice if it were a well-known fact that we know best

Perth's population in the 1970s grew as rapidly as SEQ is growing today, and a strategic crisis faced the Metropolitan Water Board (MWB). New water sources were more expensive, and an attempt was under way to connect the 100 000 houses on septic tanks to the sewer. To continue in the old way would have bankrupted the MWB. The crisis forced a strategic reappraisal, the forerunner of what is now called micro-economic reform. The mid-1970s oil crises had changed the economic climate. The environment had become a central issue, problems and their solutions were more complex. The need for dialogue with a diverse range of stakeholders was paramount — not unlike the quagmire now faced by state road authorities. The team drafting the MWB's first corporate plan had a poster on the wall: Wouldn't it be nice if it were a well-known fact that we know best. Economic and environmental necessity drove the organisation to communicate with its stakeholders, to recognise and respect other viewpoints. The corporate plans have given details of all projects that the MWB was considering *possible* in the following five years and longer. Nothing was hidden. The attitude developed that the public, the board's customers, had a right to know, to be involved. There had to be a very good reason to withhold information.

The Water Authority of WA (WAWA), the MWB's successor, recently developed strategic plans for waste-water to 2040 and water to 2050. WAWA actively sought out key stakeholders, especially its critics. They were involved in planning the consultation process and defining the issues from the outset. WAWA first published a series of information papers inviting comment, held seminars for those interested, assisted others to hold their own. The consultants told WAWA to listen and not preach in the early stages. The authority responded with its views at a later stage followed by a further round of workshops and seminars. The final outcome was a Public Environmental Report for formal assessment under the Environmental Protection Authority's statutory processes.

Had this approach been adopted in Queensland and New South Wales both SEQ and Sydney would be well on the way to solving their transport problems in an affordable way. And both Goss and Fahey would have romped home in recent elections.

The constraints of an environmentally limited resource becoming more expensive to supply are leading the water industry to focus on demand management to promote more efficient and less wasteful water use. WAWA's Perth water strategy now includes specific water efficiency programs as well as new supply proposals. Water efficiency saving programs are costed alongside proposed new source works together with the benefits to both WAWA and society (WAWA 1995). It is no longer possible to 'predict and provide'.

The drought in eastern Australia has focused attention on wise water use and recycling of some waste waters. Use of 'grey' water (from baths, showers, laundries and roof run-off) for non potable uses is firmly on the agenda, according to the president of the Institution of Engineers, Australia (Mair 1995).

The water industry, like roads, is dominated by professional engineers. They have been described philosophically as 'structuralists'; when presented with a problem the first instinct is to think of a structure as a solution, a technological fix. Water is an all-pervasive environmental agent, the source of life. Water engineers have had to adjust to this reality over the last twenty-five years. They have begun a cultural transformation yet to seriously touch the road professionals, who still persist with the predict and provide philosophy. When the latter have a problem involving transport they still think a road is the answer. But what was the question?

9
Australia's Food System: Farm to Kitchen

Australia's people are well fed and food is not too expensive. But there are latent problems that could swiftly threaten this situation early next century. Australia is a dry country, much of it desert. Furthermore, it is an ancient landscape where essential plant nutrients like phosphorus, nitrogen and key trace elements have been lost by millions of years of leaching. Biological productivity is inherently low and wrenching droughts are common. Only 8 per cent of the land is suitable for agriculture, and intensive European-style double and triple cropping is not possible. Periods of fallow are necessary. Consequently only about 3 per cent of the land can be cropped at any one time (Watt 1982).

By the end of the nineteenth century European farming methods were destroying the fragile soil structure, and crop yields fell rapidly. This century's use of fertilisers, better crop rotations and use of legumes, improved plant and animal genetic stock and the mechanisation of farming have helped to contain past land degradation and offset the inherent low biological productivity. But these innovations also enabled agriculture to expand into even more marginal land. Irrigation systems have led to more intensive farming buffered against crippling drought. Extensive use of herbicides and insecticides have been the most recent developments. This industrial agricultural system has produced its own land degradation problems, for example soil compaction from farm machinery, salination, and acidification from fertiliser use. It all requires a substantial fossil-fuel input — primarily petroleum. Cheap transport is critical to the existence of this industrial food system. Mechanisation of agriculture through use of fossil fuels, together with cheap transport, has robbed rural communities of their businesses and population, and has led to the fraying of their social fabric.

But problems are mounting. Nutrient enrichment of waterways and estuaries is causing chronic algal blooms. Land degradation continues, intensified in eastern Australia by the devastating droughts of 1983–84 and the 1990s. Salinity problems are increasing in irrigation areas and on dryland farms, especially in Western Australia. Droughts, together with competition from subsidised agriculture in Europe and the USA, are squeezing many farmers' incomes, making it difficult for them to introduce more sustainable farming practices. And the sealed rural road network now needs major reconstruction. All this when the availability and economic quality of petroleum are about to decline.

We will outline the role of fossil fuels, especially petroleum, in the industrial agriculture system. First we will examine 1974–75 energy use in our farm to kitchen food system based on a thesis by Muriel Watt, 'An Energy Analysis of the Australian Food System' (Watt 1982). We will briefly discuss changes since 1975, then the Grains Council of Australia's concerns on the economic and ecological sustainabilty of wheat production. From this we will draw some conclusions about the strategic direction of rural economic development, constrained, of course, by the ecological boundaries that shape what is possible.

Table 9.1 shows energy used in the four sectors of the food system: agriculture, food processing, retail and households. From here on households are called kitchens. Primary energy is that at the source, for example coal at the coalmine, crude oil at the well head. Delivered energy is that energy entering the sector concerned after transformation and transit losses from the primary energy source (e.g. conversion of coal to electricity). Useful energy is that energy actually used to perform work in the sector concerned, for example the actual energy needed to raise the temperature of water. The difference between delivered and useful energy represents transformation and transit losses in the sector. Embodied energy is the energy incorporated directly or indirectly in the making of vehicles, machinery, structures, fertilisers and chemicals that are used in the sector.

Table 9.1
Components of the Australian food system 1974–75 (petajoules)

Sectors	Energy			
	Embodied	*Primary*	*Delivered*	*Useful*
Agriculture	101	74	55	16.5
Food processing	63	65	45	25
Retail	16	37	30	20
Kitchen	23	188	77	33
Total	**203**	**364**	**207**	**95**

Constructed from Figures 5.10 to 5.14 and Tables 5.26, 5.33, 5.35, 5.36 in Watt 1982.

Total primary energy consumed in 1974–75 (primary plus embodied in Table 9.1) was 567 PJ, 21 per cent of total primary energy consumed in Australia.

Farms

Direct fuel, mostly distillate, was 42 per cent of farm energy use for food, including exports. Other significant energy inputs were for fertilisers (11 per cent), farm transport (12 per cent) and farm structures and equipment (17 per cent). Grain and oilseed production consumed the most energy (30 per cent), followed by cattle for meat (14 per cent, mainly transport) and sugar (9 per cent).

There is also produce waste on the farm, representing both a food and energy loss, as yet not quantified and possibly significant. Output from non irrigated agriculture can be quite variable due to climatic factors.

Food processing: exports and imports

Direct energy was the biggest primary input at 37 per cent, followed by transport (28 per cent) and packaging (26 per cent). Equipment, vehicles and buildings consumed the remainder. Road transport consumed 94 per cent of transport energy. The largest energy consumers were meat and milk processing, sugar and alcoholic beverages. Sugar mills used mainly bagasse, a substantial contribution to national primary energy at 60 PJ per annum.

There is significant wastage of food during processing, perhaps as high as 30 per cent, a significant loss of primary energy already used on the way from farm to food processor.

Retail and restaurants

Petroleum and natural gas were the main direct fuels used. Buildings, packaging and road transport were other major energy users, as were air-conditioning plants and refrigeration in supermarkets.

Kitchens

The kitchen sector is the largest user of primary energy, with refrigeration dominating. One third of all useful energy and 40 per cent of primary energy used in the food system are consumed in the kitchen. Up to 25 per cent of food is lost as kitchen and plate waste, representing a significant energy loss.

Diet

The average 1974–75 diet required 86 MJ of support energy. However, we over-eat and obesity is a problem. A nutritionally adequate diet, as recommended in 1977 by the US Senate Select Committee on Nutrition, requires only two thirds of this, or 57 MJ

(Watt 1982, p. 254). A balanced vegetarian diet has a similar support energy need. A smaller proportion of the Australian diet is from grain-fed animal products than in the USA. However, arid-range-land cattle have a high transport energy component because of distance. Hence our scope for improving food energy efficiency by reducing animal products in our diet is not as great as the USA's.

Transport

Transport consumed 88 PJ or 15 per cent of food system primary energy, including the export component, and mostly by road. This was some 14 per cent of all transport primary energy use and 20 per cent of road energy. Wheat is mostly carted to coastal markets by rail.

Comment

A change of diet, less food waste in the kitchen and in food processing, together with improved energy efficiency in kitchens are the principal areas for improving fossil-fuel energy efficiency in the Australian food system. Since 1974–75 the population has increased by one third, cotton production tenfold, red meat production has stabilised and consumption declined. Wheat production has declined, but grain consumption has increased. Per capita milk, vegetable and fruit production is virtually unchanged. Sugar production has increased, but per capita consumption decreased. The area of farms has decreased from 500 to 460 million hectares since 1974–75. Some marginal areas and degraded land have been abandoned, especially since the 1983–84 drought. Some have been swallowed up by urban growth and hobby farms (Newman et al. 1994, pp. 51, 70).

Kitchen energy use since 1974–75 may have decreased due to the use of natural gas, microwave ovens and consumption of fast foods. The latter has probably increased energy use in the retail sector. It is not clear what changes may have occurred elsewhere, there are pluses and minuses on the energy front. An update of Watt's thesis is highly desirable.

The longer the food chain from farm to kitchen the more steps in the chain where energy transformation losses occur, and the less energy efficient the system becomes. Long food chains have fewer opportunities for recycling packaging, and the more packaging is needed the harder it is to recycle food wastes. The first real stresses on this system are going to come where oil is the key energy source. These are transport, farm tractors, fertilisers and farm chemicals. The pressure will be on to bring food consumers closer to farmers so that use of energy for food processing and packaging is reduced, and the transport chain for recycling of packages is shortened.

Big Ben Pies has one automated factory in Sydney supplying all of Australia except the Northern Territory (pers. comm., 15 June 1994).

Enterprises of this kind will not survive shrinking high-quality oil supplies. Pies should be made locally in a labour-intensive way.

Howard Croxon, president of the WA Road Transport Association (Inc.), in an address to the Perth FAFTR 1994 Summit had this to say:

> The road system throughout this state is undoubtedly our lifeline. We are dependent on goods reaching us from the eastern states by road ... Let me take you through this process by using the humble baked bean.

> There are transport costs associated with the manufacturing process to produce a can of them. The cans join others in a box. The box, when filled, is transported to a warehouse where it is stored waiting for orders. An order comes in from Western Australia and the box is transported to a depot where it joins other produce, similarly packaged, for shipment by road to Perth.

> It arrives in Perth by road train. The road train, because of its size, is divided into smaller units outside Perth and the trailer containing our humble cartons of baked beans is moved to a depot in a Perth suburb. It is then moved to a food distribution outlet where it is stored, awaiting another order. The order arrives and the box containing baked beans is loaded on to, you guessed it, a truck, where it is delivered to a supermarket. (Croxon 1994)

No wonder baked beans are expensive! How much more expensive if we go on a splurge of national highway and freeway expansion and then find fuel is scarce and prohibitively expensive! In February 1995 a flood blocked the Eyre Highway on the Nullarbor Plain for three weeks. Two trucks held up on each side of the flood were both carrying carrots!

Wheat in crisis

Australia is the world's fourth-largest wheat exporting country and has a low-cost production system able so far to deliver unsubsidised grain to the world, but with considerable environmental consequences. Wheat exports from the USA and Canada are subsidised. Some 96 out of 520 million tonnes of world wheat production was traded annually in the four years to 1991–92. Australian growers export 10 million tonnes per year, 70 per cent of the crop. Market prospects for wheat are good.

On the surface wheat farms are in good condition. However, a Grains Council of Australia report, *Inventing the Future*, says the industry is at a critical juncture. Plantings and production are well down on their 1983–84 peak. Many wheat farmers and their farms are exhausted, in terms of both soils and finances; they no longer have the strength to withstand repeated blows such as the current drought. There is a real question mark over the long-term economic and agronomic sustainability of the industry (Grains Council 1995, p. 1).

Wheat farmers have experienced a steady price fall of wheat from A$400 per tonne in 1960 to under A$200 per tonne in 1990 (1988 dollars). Subsidised agriculture overseas has contributed to these wheat price declines. A large part of *Inventing the Future* discusses cost-reduction options, markets, marketing problems, transport and grain-handling issues, including the impact of deregulation on these. These marketing questions will not be discussed here, important as they are, but rather the ecological problems of our wheat farmers. Nevertheless, falling prices are part of these latter problems, and the economic capacity of farmers to solve them is adversely affected.

As already stated Australia's erosion-prone and nutrient-deficient soils have low biological productivity, dramatically illustrated in Figure 9.1 which compares international wheat yields. We have the lowest yields per hectare and these have been static since 1960 whereas the rest of the world's crop yield has improved. Heavy government subsidies have supported high fertiliser use to increase European yields, and the US situation has already been discussed. The introduction of hybrid seeds linked to artificial fertiliser use has lifted Indian and Chinese crop yields and created the so called 'green revolution'. More people than ever are thus dependent on food production arising from fossil-fuel-based productivity gains.

Figure 9.1

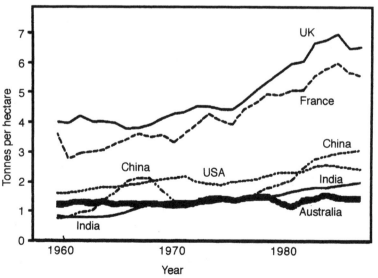

INTERNATIONAL WHEAT YIELDS

Note: Three year central moving average

Grains Council 1995: Milling Wheat Project, Inventing the Future, p. 33

Figure 9.2

PROTEIN DECLINE OVER THE LAST 60 YEARS

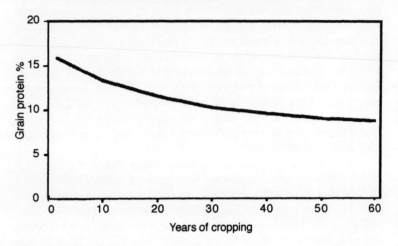

Grains Council 1995: Milling Wheat Project, Inventing the Future, p. 33

Equally serious is the decline in grain protein on land cropped over a long period of time, as shown in Figure 9.2 — a clear indication of unsustainable farm practices. It is high-protein wheats that command a premium price.

Consequently the Australian Wheat Board has launched a '2 x 10 x 2000' campaign to increase yields to 2 tonnes per hectare and protein to 10 per cent by the year 2000. However, improvements are limited by climate, rainfall, soil quality, genetics and management expertise. It is not clear whether these barriers can all be overcome. Many growers have decided the answer is no. The area sown to wheat has declined by 27 per cent over the last ten years, mostly in Queensland and New South Wales where the decline has been 40 per cent. The droughts of 1982–83 and the 1990s have been an important factor. These percentages may improve again as the drought ends (Grains Council 1995, p. 33).

The report says researchers have solutions but these are likely to be expensive and risky for individual growers. More sophisticated farm management is seen as an important tool, and measurement of inputs and outputs to more finely hone performance. However, pasture legumes do not generate comparable incomes, especially with low wool prices. Higher protein seed varieties might cost more and quantitative farm management is more labour-intensive. Heavy fertiliser use can increase costs but can be completely wasted if the weather is unfavourable, and has other soil-damaging effects. According to

Figure 9.3

ANNUAL FERTILISER CONSUMPTION IN AUSTRALIA

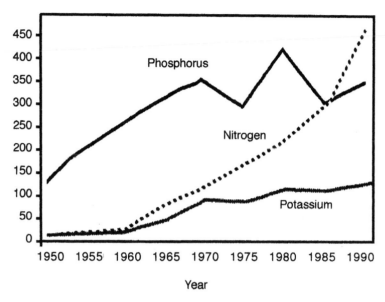

Grains Council 1995: Milling Wheat Project, Inventing the Future, p. 32

ABARE data many cereal farmers may not be financially strong enough to invest in new practices and varieties. Widely fluctuating farm profit and growing farm debt have brought estimated farm debts to $12 billion. Under some pessimistic trade forecasts a significant number of cereal farmers will be economically unsustainable by 2000 (Grains Council 1995, p. 34).

Fertilisers have played a key role in offsetting nutrient-poor soils for our agriculture this century. Figure 9.3 shows Australia's annual fertiliser consumption. A dramatic twenty-fold increase in nitrogen fertiliser use has occurred since 1965. Fossil fuels are needed for fertiliser manufacture — 1500–2500 MJ per tonne for superphosphate, depending on the sulphur source for sulphuric acid. However, nitrogen fertilisers use natural gas or petroleum as a feedstock and had an energy intensity of 37 000 MJ per tonne in 1980 (Watt 1982, p. 177). For 1990 this was equivalent to 0.5–0.8 PJ primary energy for superphosphate and 16.5 PJ for nitrogen fertilisers, 2 per cent of natural gas production.

Sugar cane and vegetable growing consume significant amounts of nitrogen fertiliser. Chemicals and fertilisers make up more than half the input costs in all wheat-growing regions. Farmers are increasing fertiliser use to improve income through higher yield and protein; the benefit is still greater than the cost (Grains Council 1995, p. 32), but for how long? The Grains Council did not consider the future avail-ability and economics of petroleum supplies as an issue in its report.

Climate shifts may be partly responsible for the contraction of Queensland and New South Wales wheat production. Between 1881 and 1940 arid zones in South Australia and New South Wales moved 200 kilometres nearer the coast. However, since World War II New South Wales wheat growing has extended some 200 kilometres further inland and the 200 millimetre rainfall line has also moved inland the same distance. Do the recent droughts herald a return to a drier phase in south-eastern Australia?

Severe droughts in eastern and northern Australia are associated with the Pacific Ocean climatic phenomenon called El Nino. It varies in intensity and frequency. Two of the recent El Nino-driven droughts have been particularly severe; the last devastated wheat production. We became heavily dependent for local needs on Western Australian production, normally one third of the country's total. In 1995 we came close to importing wheat for stockfeed — pigs and poultry. However, the West Australian wheat-belt is also under several threats. First, soils there are particularly nutrient-deficient, especially in phosphorus, and wheat growing would collapse without the use of superphosphate. Second, winter rainfall has declined 22 per cent since 1930 (*Ecos* 1992), especially in the more marginal north-east. But the biggest threat comes from salination and other soil problems like compaction from farm machinery and acidification.

Western Australia's south-west is a salinised landscape. Ocean salt in the rain is high, as are evapotranspiration losses. The proportion of rain reaching rivers is low. Consequently, significant salt has accumu-lated in the subsoil and deeper ground waters, except in the wetter parts. The original perennial vegetation kept the salt at bay, and infil-trating rain was consumed by vegetation at shallow depths or reached rivers as fresh water. Clearing of the land for agriculture has reduced transpiration water losses and led to a slow rise of saline ground waters. Hence half the river-stream flow has become saline or brackish this century. More is at risk. Increasing areas of farmland are being salinised and lost to production in an over-cleared landscape. Salt affected 443 000 hectares in 1989, with 2 447 000 hectares potentially at risk (Select Committee 1991). In five river basins a licence from the Water Authority of Western Australia is required to chop down trees. The Water Authority is selectively buying back farms and revegetating the Collie River basin in a so far successful attempt to reduce saline flows into Wellington dam.

Soil acidity threatens the productivity of nearly 10 million hectares of Western Australia's wheat-belt, according to a national report by the

Land and Water Research and Development Corporation. Soil acidity leads to declining yields and eventually soil infertility. It is caused by the removal of plant material through grazing, harvesting or hay-cutting, leaching of nitrogen from fertilisers and legume crops, and the use of ammonium-based fertilisers (*West Australian* 1995). Spreading lime on affected soils is one way of restoring the pH balance. The report says rates of lime use will need to increase by 500 per cent to sustainably improve acidic soils over the next fifty years. But farmers say the cost of lime is a barrier — another fossil-fuel input with a high transport component. The Western Australian Department of Agriculture is holding farmer workshops on the topic.

The Landcare movement originating in the late-1980s struck deeper roots among wheat-belt farmers in Western Australia than elsewhere. A vigorous community-based movement to re-establish deep-rooted perennial vegetation on farms is emerging, a recognition that agricultural practices must change and much of the landscape restored to woodland in strategic locations to contain salination. The movement is backed up by a professional research establishment who are world leaders in dryland salination. It is a desperate race against time in the more critical areas.

A Legislatve Assembly Select Committee into Land Conservation, chaired by Monty House MLA, now Minister for Agriculture, comprehensively studied these Western Australian land and environment degradation problems (Select Committee 1991). It recommended that the solutions needed to have a strong community base for enduring success, a base that had to include the urban population. City schools are developing associations with rural Landcare groups. The schools propagate the tree seedlings and in May each year the children take them to the country and share with farmers and others the task of planting them out. A cultural transformation is beginning.

Industrial agriculture and cheap transport have robbed these rural communities of their population to such an extent that many are at the point of desperation. The suicide rate is high. Will the era of declining oil quality and availability see people return to rural communities?

These socially and economically weakened rural communities need help on many fronts to cope with these enormous problems. Our self sufficiency in wheat during future El Nino-induced droughts could be at risk. However, these farmers, their professional advisers and most people have yet to realise the need to look *beyond oil* in their plans for a different agriculture.

The limited high-quality petroleum fuels remaining are critical over the next two decades for the successful reconstruction of a sustainable farming environment that can survive, first with limited use of oil and ultimately with none.

Wheat growing may only be possible on a limited scale. If so what are the alternative crop systems compatible with poor soils, climate and salinised landscapes; what transport systems are appropriate? At least the farming community and some urban dwellers are beginning to search for new ways. Many are experimenting and probing new ground. These rural communities cannot carry out the task by themselves in the limited time available, they need considerable help from the rest of the community, help that will require the use of fossil fuels, especially oil. The decisive energy-intensive steps must be taken within twenty years. Beyond then, not only the quantity but also the economic quality of remaining petroleum will be deteriorating, making the transition task more difficult.

Australia's soil degradation problem is almost certainly far more serious than the USA's because of our climate and inherently poor soils. From this perspective the transport priorities of Cox and Allen Consulting in downgrading rural roads in favour of urban freeways seem bizarre. They forget that people can only eat food, not GDP. The current drive to build urban freeways, motorways and tollways is an economic obscenity. Our urban populations must consume less oil as fast as they can. Alternatives are available to them that are not so readily available to rural communities. Much of the oil that city transport now consumes will be needed for food production.

Like the USA, Australia too needs to give agriculture and rural communities the first priority for oil supplies. We will not be able to have our oil and eat it too.

10

Conclusion

James Watt's improvements to the steam engine 200 years ago ushered in the modern era powered by fossil fuels. First there was coal, then oil, followed by natural gas. Fifty years passed before inventive geniuses had accumulated enough advances in metallurgy and engineering to enable the age of steam to 'take-off'. From 1840 steam-powered railways and ships significantly increased the scope of transport and lowered its cost. Each innovation stimulated further expansion and innovation in an ever-expanding cycle, unrestrained by limits to the supply of coal. One hundred and fifty years' growth of population, cities and centralised production began to serve global markets.

Colonel Drake drilled the first oil well in Pennsylvania in 1859. Another forty years of invention led to the internal combustion engine and the beginning of powered road transport and aviation. World War II saw the decisive triumph of petroleum-powered transport over coal-fired steam for rail and shipping. Rapid expansion of electric power grids and industrial agriculture began. US fears of petroleum shortages in World War II, along with the invention of welded steel pipelines, saw the first systematic marketing of natural gas, previously flared at oil fields as a waste product. Natural gas has been the growth fuel since the mid-1960s.

Fossil fuels at the climax

The first of these fossil fuels, oil, is passing through its Hubbert peak. Natural gas will be next by the middle of next century. Published reports of coal reserves speak of more than 200 years availability, ignoring restraints that may be imposed by the greenhouse effect. It may therefore seem a strange suggestion that we are already at the climax of the fossil-fuel age.

This judgment involves more than fuel quantity. Economic quality is involved as well. EPR is one vital factor to consider. But, above all, on a joule for joule basis oil is economically more effective than coal — the fuel-type argument of chapter 1. In chapter 6 we saw that both declining quantity and quality of oil in the USA will soon lead to a decline in GDP per capita. All alternative measures to offset the economic consequences of this decline are overwhelmed by both the reduced availability and quality of oil as the supreme economically effective fossil fuel. Less wealth can be generated in oil's declining phase. Natural gas occupies an intermediate position between coal and oil, it is more expensive to store and transport because it is a gas. This fact limits the scope for gas to replace oil in our present transport system and in industrial agriculture. The first step towards a better world is to face this reality.

Furthermore, the economic effectiveness of coal, gas and electricity as we now use them is critically dependent on the low-cost, flexible and highly connective transport system that we have. It runs almost exclusively on oil. The transport system carts raw materials, intermediate products and services to and between manufacturing plants, and carts finished goods to final customers. Transport is needed for recycling and waste disposal. Declining oil will force structural changes that both reduce our energy use and the size and availability of our highly networked and extensive transport systems. Improving energy efficiency at each stage of the existing production and distribution chain will not be enough, though very necessary and long overdue in Australia.

Harnessing these fossil fuels to human labour has permitted a massive exploitation of natural resources to serve human ends, now occurring on a scale threatening the fabric of the living world. This level of exploitation cannot continue without reducing the capacity of the planet to support the present human population, let alone any increase.

Finally, only a few nations, perhaps 20 per cent of the world's population, have had the privilege of participating in this fossil-fuel bonanza, namely North America, Europe, Japan and a few minor ones like Australia and New Zealand. Now the industrialising Asians, Indians and Latin Americans are staking a massive claim on oil precisely when it is near its Hubbert peak. These newcomers will not be able to reach the oil-based heights we have — the high-quality resource base needed simply does not exist. Nor can we continue with the high energy-consuming systems that we now have. The USA, Canada and Australia have the world's most energy-intensive and oil-dependent economies. Australia alone among developed nations has failed to improve its overall energy efficiency since the 1970s.

The uneven global distribution of oil and gas resources reinforces the significance of this historic transition. The major western oil companies and those nations which have had privileged access to oil have been losing their century-long control of the resource since the mid-1970s. Other nations quite rightly want a greater share, and will succeed in gaining it. The need for us to change our ways has never been more urgent. The combination of these reasons means that we are at the climax of the fossil-fuel age.

What are the implications?

Young people have the least to gain by continuation of our present high-energy consumption system, and most to lose if we fail to change in time.

Australians, like US citizens, face a reduction in per capita wealth. Indeed it may already be happening. Part of the population is already experiencing a decline in access to consumption, and young people, reacting to a lack of prospects, are the focus of growing concerns from their elders.

Studies along the lines of that carried out by the Complex Systems Research Center at the University of New Hampshire are needed to confirm this decline (Gever et al. 1991). Our Hubbert peak for oil is coming later than for the USA, but our oil fields are smaller and mostly offshore, and will decline faster than the USA's. However, we are a net exporter of energy (coal and natural gas) and have yet to deplete our high-grade minerals — short-term mitigating circumstances by comparison with the USA. But we also have more severe degradation of agricultural lands that need urgent rehabilitation, as discussed for wheat production. Neither will we be immune to events in the rest of the world.

We urgently need to know the EPR profiles of our coal, oil and gas resources since their exploitation began. How do these profiles compare with those elsewhere and what are the future EPR prospects for these fuels? We need to assess the urgency of the situation we face; how fast we need to change.

It is no longer feasible to increase productivity by a general substitution of energy and capital for labour, reversing the pattern existing for over 150 years. The declining quantity and economic quality of oil tends to work against it. Capital investment, itself an energy-consuming activity, has been the means to harness abundant high-quality energy to labour. Some productivity gains are still possible by improving the energy efficiency of existing commerce and industry as a step towards more fundamental structural change.

The future belongs to more labour-intensive operations, not general use of automated plant. It is time to question the wisdom of generous tax-depreciation allowances for industrial plant and equipment while penalising labour with payroll taxes. Productivity gains by employers and employees alike are becoming more elusive as availability of the high-quality petroleum fuels responsible for past gains fades. In wage bargaining these days working conditions are often traded for pay increases without a net gain to workers. Simultaneous high employment and high earnings are no longer possible, nor can we expect continuous increases in incomes. On the other hand some businesses are exploring new ways of managing to cope with the new environment, sharing management with their work force, and developing cooperative relations with other businesses. These are among the more effective ways to improve energy efficiency.

Depletion of high-quality resources leads to the substitution of low waged labour for high-waged labour and a low-return rate for high-return-rate capital. Therefore natural resource scarcity reduces the material content of the lifestyles of wage earner and stockholder alike, but not evenly (Hall, Cleveland & Kaufmann 1986, p. ix). Declining oil quality erodes the possibility of economic growth; we have to run faster just to stay where we are. The present false summer of low oil prices is allowing the old system to continue beyond its use by date, consuming the precious high-quality oil needed for a comfortable transition to the new. These trends are appearing as high unemployment, especially among youth and older unskilled workers. A polarisation of wealth in the community is occurring. Crime and poverty are increasing, as are drug addiction and social stress. Social justice, equity and democracy issues are sharpening.

The next generation will have less mobility, less freedom to travel. Hitherto, developed countries could cater for all oil-consuming activities. In the decades ahead difficult choices will need to be made, and some oil uses will have to be forgone or curtailed to accommodate oil's use in essential sectors such as agriculture. Transport is the biggest consumer of oil. To survive, our cities must shift swiftly to more fuel-efficient public transport systems, not powered by oil, to reduce the need for both business and private travel. New roads and rail systems last for decades, well into the coming economic era. Transport infrastructure strategies now need to look *beyond oil*. This reverses the pattern of the past 200 years, in which transport has undergone continuous expansion and cost reduction. The unrealistic thrust for a global economy, as expressed in the GATT negotiations and the new World Trade Organisation, will quickly confront this transport obstacle. Greater local self sufficiency will necessarily follow as global markets contract.

The food system must become less energy-intensive, less dependent on petroleum as an integral part of a major community-based commitment to quickly reverse land degradation, and adapting to an agriculture that conserves land fertility and which can survive beyond oil. A shift to more labour-intensive practices and away from monoculture is implied — the key to coping with drought. Cheap fuel and transport have robbed rural communities of their population, industries and businesses. Urban food consumers and farmers have to come closer together, to reduce the length of the food chain. What transport systems are appropriate to this new world? What fuels will provide the motive power? There are opportunities here for the reinvigoration of rural communities.

A very large proportion of the world's population depends for food from high agricultural yields achieved by the use of fossil fuels. The world may only be able to support a population of 3 billion without this input (Hall, Cleveland & Kaufmann 1986, p. 139). Petroleum is a key fuel. We have discussed food systems in the USA and Australia. The principal grain exporters are the USA, Canada, Europe, Australia and Argentina — all highly dependent on petroleum-based industrial agriculture.

Will we see an end to urban growth during the twenty-first century, a contraction of megacities? Some will argue that alternative energy sources can replace petroleum fuels, especially for road transport. It is too late for undiscovered energy sources. It takes decades to bring them into significant commercial production. Those alternative sources to oil already known or in use require large investments for their production, storage, and distribution systems, and to make the engines needed to use the new fuels.

We saw in chapter 5 that these alternative fuels have low EPRs compared with the last fifty years of oil. For many the initial energy cost for their introduction is high. Consequently the investment required to introduce them would be immense, take years, and be additional to that required to produce the remaining oil. It would be an additional drain on petroleum supplies declining in availability and economic effectiveness. Many uses would have to be sacrificed.

The important alternative energy investments for the transition must be commenced before the declining quantity and quality of petroleum production begins to drag the economy downhill. It is net energy that matters. Remaining high-quality oil and gas are needed to facilitate an easy transition. For Australia this means a rapidly closing ten to twenty year period. Otherwise the energy industry may become like a black hole sucking the rest of the economy into it.

This contrasts with the transition from coal to oil earlier this century. Converting ships to oil-firing was easy: add an oil injector to the boiler, convert coalbunkers to oil storage, construct storage tanks at ports. These were the highly productive years of oil. Less labour was needed. The shift from steam locomotives to diesel electric saved railways an immense burden in carting coal and supplying water for locomotives. Frequent stops to refuel and take on water were eliminated and the real cost of transport was reduced.

These issues are particularly important for the superannuation industry and its clients. Superannuation is a long-term strategic investment to provide financial security during the contributors' retirement, for many thirty, forty years ahead. The changing fortunes of oil will dramatically alter the viable investments and expected rates-of-return over the next forty years. It is critically important that the super industry anticipates the changing environment, thinks *beyond oil* and shifts investments to those areas with a viable future, away from those that will not survive. The superannuation industry and its clients have a vital interest in such a new investment strategy and must be a party to its development. Energy analyses of the kind pioneered by Odum and Costanza have a vital role to play.

Professional elitism and bureaucracy: playing at being God

In AD 640 the Caliph Omar invaded Egypt and destroyed the famous Library of Alexandria, ending a book-copying industry hundreds of years old. During the invasion the library's scholars were conducting esoteric debates on how many angels could dance on the point of a needle. Today thirty year traffic forecasts and cost-benefit studies for urban roads have the character of these ancient scholarly debates. They are not grounded in the real world. How can this happen in the modern world?

To help answer this question we need to look, if only briefly, at a very complex question: the origins of the system of ideas underlying modern thought. Scientists today are wrestling with the realisation that observers are always interacting with the subjects under investigation. For most, this is still novel. But go back 400 years to the victory of the idea that sunrise and sunset are due to the rotation of the earth, and the seasons to its inclination and orbit around the sun. Along with this there emerged a view that everything works like a rational, harmonious clockwork mechanism, a lifeless automaton. Galileo and Descartes were early architects of this model. The culmination was Isaac Newton's laws of motion, published on the eve of England's Glorious Revolution in 1688. These ideas have had a pervasive influence in shaping the world over the last 300 years, especially western political, government, academic, professional and business institutions.

Newton's work is rarely read in full, rarely analysed in its social context. His rational mechanics envisaged an independent observer located in absolute space of infinite and homogeneous dimensions. Bodies in this perfect geometrical space could be exactly measured in pure mathematical time. All events past, present and future could be observed in their totality. Nothing was uncertain. To Newton both the observer and these absolute space and time entities were the everlasting omnipresence of Almighty God. An activist God whose attributes combined the mathematical order and harmony of the world with the traditional ones of His absolute dominion and wilful control of events. Absolute space for Newton is not only the omnipresence of God; it is also the infinite scene of divine knowledge and control (Burtt 1932, pp. 254–60). Hence all real motion in the last analysis comes from an expenditure of *eternal divine energy*. Thus Newton considered the independent observer in absolute space to be God, the rational all-seeing, all-knowing, all-powerful law-giving God of Judaeo Christianity. The scientist became God. There is no room here for choice or free will by ordinary people. Newton's followers enthusiastically accepted his laws of motion, but soon discarded his theology — or thought they had. The ghost of God remained as the independent absolutely rational objective observer *outside* the phenomenon under investigation. From being accidents of a living God, events became sheer, fixed, geometrical measures of the mechanical motions of masses. And this loss of their divinity completed the despiritualisation of nature, a dead world. In this world people are just lumps of meat interacting according to some deadly version of Newton's laws.

Furthermore, the agenda was nothing less than bringing the whole of nature under control, and playing at being God. This ethos pervades the culture of contemporary professions and bureaucracies, both government and non government. It is also reflected in the behaviour of mainstream political parties and governments. A small minority are aware of the theological overtones. However, most would be surprised, even hurt, to be told they are playing at being God. This belief as part of our cultural heritage is the source of much authoritarian and arrogant behaviour, exploited by narrow vested interests to give their agendas respectability.

Traffic forecasts, for example, can assume an aura of unchallengeable manifest destiny. The forecasting methods use elaborate mathematics to describe the travel behaviour of people interacting in networks like unthinking lumps of meat. Road agencies and governments then go to devious lengths to impose their vision on a hostile public by stealth. This behaviour, of course, is not unique to road agencies or governments.

Wouldn't it be nice if it were a well-known fact that we know best!

Newton's mechanical philosophy provided justification for the absolute monarchies of his day, the divine right of kings. Elements of this absolutism still survive in our Westminster system of government.

J.R. Saul, in his book *Voltaire's Bastards: The Dictatorship of Reason in the West*, argues that these rationalist modes of thought from the past have become deeply destructive forces in the public life of the West (Saul 1992).

He says:

> Human affairs are now dominated by an ideology of blind reason, which separates the exercise of reason from intuition, from common experience, from the memory of past events and experiments, and above all from values — ethical and moral considerations that arise from complex organic relationships among ourselves and with nature.

These ethical and moral values are profoundly shaped by community experiences, environmental constraints and boundaries, as well as by the use and abuse of power. These values are central to the survival of the global ecosystems upon which we all depend.

He says this dictatorship of reason is exercised by a largely anonymous elite, located in government, business and the tertiary sector and manipulated from time to time by politicians or demagogues in an almost unrestrained pursuit of power. Vested interests are able to manipulate this rationality to further their own ends. The fatal flaw, the 'grave misunderstanding at the heart of reason', was the assumption that it was a moral force. In fact the structured application of rational procedures is neutral with respect to ends and as often applied to advance evil and destructive purposes as it is to promote the good. (Sheehan 1994)

Recall our discussion in chapter 7 on Cox's use of the ORANI economic model with its thousand assumptions requiring value judgments by the modeller. These judgments rightly belong to the community.

New science, the re-enchantment of nature: an end to elitism

The divine myth at the heart of classical science has always been under challenge. The Frenchman Diderot was a vociferous eighteenth-century critic, as was Mary Shelley some years later in her novel, *Frankenstein*.

The first cracks in this edifice appeared in the nineteenth century with the development of the science of energy and the concept of entropy as the irreversible dissipation of free energy into an unavailable form. A challenge to the timelessness of mechanics and its vision of *eternal divine energy* that is never used up.

Early in the twentieth century Einstein abandoned absolute space, and quantum mechanics abandoned absolute determinism. The future was recognised to have many possibilities not totally predictable in advance. Furthermore, in the quantum model, the visions and beliefs of scientists were recognised to be a part of scientific observations through the design of experiments and measuring apparatus. The values, belief systems and expectations of scientists are an integral part of the science that develops. They are no longer neutral, rational, objective observers in the Newtonian sense, but embedded *within* nature and society. Scientists began to become human; no longer Gods. However, old mechanistic beliefs still have a strong grip on all our minds, sustained by institutional inertia, vested interests and above all by the unrecognised values embodied in the Newtonian mechanical viewpoint.

The Newtonian vision is now recognised as valid only under conditions at or near *thermodynamic equilibrium*, conditions that are rare and fragile. There is negligible energy flow, hence negligible information exchange; connections between the whole and its parts are weak. Such systems are static, they never evolve. Equilibrium leads to death.

Prigogine and Stengers have recognised that the universe we live in is overwhelmingly 'far from thermodynamic equilibrium', and vastly different from the mechanical world of Newton. An open dynamic world of free energy flows and therefore of creative potential, not the dictatorship of absolute certainty. Entities can 'self organise' into dynamic forms, 'dissipative structures', in the words of Prigogine and Stengers, because they can only come into being and continue to exist by dissipating free energy. This is a form of metabolic activity: we are in the domain that includes evolving, living organisms and social structures such as cities. Many outcomes are possible, not always predictable in advance. Choices can and must be made, but constrained by the free energy available from nature and by ecological boundaries.

In the self organising mode there is *coherent participative behaviour* of the self organising entities, with a high level of information exchange, necessary for the generation and survival of these dynamic structures, for example the development of a fully formed foetus from a single fertilised cell. Information exchanges regulate energy flows and maintain group coherence and adaptability. The whole as well as being the sum of its parts is also the outcome of their interactions. Insignificant events can have an importance and influence out of proportion to their scale. Complexity, dynamic organisation and communication are therefore *inherent* distinguishing features (Prigogine & Stengers 1984).

Gregoire Nicolis, one of Prigogine's co-workers, says that:

> Living systems function definitely under conditions far away from equilibrium ... Adaptation and plasticity, two basic features of non

linear dynamical systems, also rank among the most conspicuous characteristics of human societies. It is therefore natural to expect that dynamical models allowing for evolution and change should be the most adequate ones for social systems. A dynamical model of a human society begins with the realisation that, in addition to its internal structure, the system is firmly embedded in an environment with which it exchanges matter, energy, and information. (Nicolis 1992)

This is far removed from the dead mechanical world of Newton. Nature has become alive, re-enchanted. People are no longer lumps of meat, or trees just pieces of wood.

Great changes are upon us. How can we ensure that people not only can cope but are also themselves the confident and assured instruments of change? How can we ensure that the needed changes are fair and just? Without justice it will not be possible to make swift and radical change and still maintain social cohesion. There will be hard and even stressful choices to make. A caring and all-inclusive way is needed; the more caring we are the more hardnosed we can be. The vision of an enchanted world now emerging in science points the way:

- Human society can never be dominant over nature, only embedded within a living environment with which it exchanges matter, energy, and information; a subordinate part of a larger world, limited by and totally dependent on it.

- Active ongoing citizen participation and interaction in the conduct of government and administration is fundamental for viable, adaptive 'self organising' energy-efficient social orders. Fair and equitable access to resources and information with minimum secrecy is required for this to happen.

- Justice, equity, moral and ethical values are of central importance. Excessive growth and concentration of arbitrary power and influence can be likened to a form of societal cancer. Issues and processes of accountability are important for social control of power flows.

- The prime roles of professionals, experts and bureaucracies are to facilitate citizen participation in decisions and management, not to control in the Godlike belief that 'we know best'. The experts' task is to help evaluate the outcomes and consequences of alternatives and help identify the value judgments and ethical choices involved. It is the citizens' role to pass judgment on these values and preferred outcomes.

- Issues are inherently complex and non linear and cannot be individually assessed in isolation. The complexity arises from the many interconnections between issues. There is no 'right answer', rather multiple open ended choices based on incomplete knowledge. The complexity is inherently beyond the capacity of any one person or agency to comprehend, it requires the collective knowledge and wisdom of everyone. If nobody is in command then everybody is.

- All these features are strongly interdependent.

Most important is an enhancement of the democratic process. We can call upon all the advances of modern communications for the active participation of people in the key decision-making processes required, indeed this is essential to success. There must be less secrecy in government, and an end to commercial confidentiality in major contracts that have significant environmental and social impacts.

We should not despair if the old institutions and power structures seem formidable and all powerful; they are not. Never have they been under such powerful challenges. The new is emerging everywhere. The enormous interest in nature and wildlife, the emerging vision of the earth as a living planet, a part of the re-enchantment of nature in western culture: the schoolchildren of Perth who grow tree seedlings and take them to the wheat-belt to help revegetate the land; the Landcare people; the global outrage at the resumption of nuclear testing by the French government; the way the *Moving Melbourne* report was produced; the way water agencies are moving away from the 'we know best' outlook.

There is also the way the Brazilian industrialist Ricardo Semler runs his manufacturing businesses: all major corporate decisions are taken by a vote of the employees, who have full access to the company accounts and increasingly are deciding their own pay rates. The company is a Brazilian success story.

All these strands worldwide are coalescing into a new global vision, of learning to live within nature's limits, of rejoicing in the magnificence of the living world's richness and diversity and recognising that we are all an integral part of it. More modest and realistic expectations of what is achievable in the future do not necessarily mean a lesser quality of life, but quite the reverse.

The scientific method began with the Greeks in the fourth century BC. Codifying of western ethics dates from the same time when myths and legends handed down orally for millennia were compiled into the familiar form of the Old Testament by Ezra the scribe. Chapter 3 in Genesis, the Fall, characterises humankind 'we are dust', that is recycled earth; and we live by the 'sweat of our face', by the exercise of our own mental and physical powers.

All our modern science confirms the ancient wisdom, technology and value judgments go together. The illusion of miracles and unlimited free gifts from nature were spawned by the too rapid unlocking of the earth's reserve treasures, a new Fall. We must be well down the path of change to reduce oil dependence during the first decade of the new century. The global day of reckoning will soon be upon us and those nations not prepared will suffer greatly.

References

Aerospace Industries Association of America Inc. 1992, *Aerospace Facts and Figures 1992–93*, pp. 79, 85.

Age 1981, 'Rundle Leaves a Policy Chasm', 8 April, p. 13.

—— 1995, 'Kennett Gives Green Light to $1.7b City Link', 30 May, p. 1.

—— 1995a, 'Freeway Toll Cheats Will be Fined, Kennett Warns', 26 July, p. 3.

—— 1995b, 'Icons on Road to Future', 1 August, p. 1.

—— 1995c, 'State to Invest $247m in Road Link Project', 1 August, p. 4.

Allen Consulting Group 1993, *Land Transport Infrastructure*, Australian Automobile Association, Canberra.

Allinson, G. 1995, 'Economics of Petroleum Exploration', *Oil & Gas Australia*, February, p. 50.

Arthur Andersen & Co. 1992, *World Oil Trends*, Arthur Andersen & Co. and Cambridge Energy Associates, pp. 1–2

Auditor-General 1994, *Private Participation in the Provision of Public Infrastructure*, NSW Auditor-General, Sydney, October.

Australian 1994, 'Lower Oil Price Hits North West Shelf', 17 February, p. 20.

—— 1994a, 'Passengers Set to Quadruple', 17 February, p. 32.

—— 1994b, 'Public Left in Dark Over Early Plan for Freeway', 12–13 November, p. 13.

—— 1994c, 'Airlines Start Climb Back From $16bn Run of Losses', 30 December, p. 26.

—— 1995, 'Cutbacks Still on Boeing's Horizon', 27 January, p. 23.

—— 1995b, 'Goss May Abandon Tollway Plan', 1 August, p. 8.

—— 1995c, 'Transurban Floats Toll Road Project', 1 August, p. 59.

Australian Bureau of Agricultural and Resource Economics (ABARE) 1993, *Energy: Demand and Supply Projections, Australia 1992–93 to 2004–5*, ABARE, Canberra.

——— 1995, *Australian Energy Consumption and Production to 2009–10*, ABARE, Canberra.

Australian Financial Review 1994, 'Weak Prices Threat to Exploration Plans', 11 January, p. 17.

——— 1994a, 'Oil Expected to Stay Cheap for Years as Market Dictates Price', 3 March, p. 23.

——— 1994b, 'Woodside Faces Profit Plunge as Oil Prices Fall', 3 March, p. 25.

——— 1994c, 'Officer Basin up for Grabs', 22 March, p. 27.

——— 1994d, 'M2 Funding Breakthrough', 29 August, p. 30.

——— 1994e, 'Funds Run Risks of the Road', 30 August, p. 52.

——— 1994f, 'High Anxiety as Carriers Keep Old Planes Flying', 7 November, p. 18.

——— 1994g, 'The End of the Road for Cars', 11 November, p. 19.

——— 1995, 'Reverse Trend Shocks Big Three Makers', 3 May p. 12.

——— 1995a, 'The Wage Squeeze', 10 July, p. 16.

Australian Institute of Petroleum (AIP) 1992, *Australia's Oil Industry*, AIP, Melbourne.

Australian Minerals and Energy Council (AMEC) 1991, *The Outlook for Crude Oil Supply and Demand in Australia and its Energy Policy Implications*, AMEC Working Party Report, AGPS, Canberra.

Australian Petroleum Exploration Association (APEA), Media Statement, APEA, Canberra, 22 January.

Austroads 1994, *Road Facts: An Overview of Australia's Road System*, Austroads, Sydney.

Bessarab, R. & Newman, P. 1993, *The Energy/GDP Relationship: Guidelines for a more sustainable economy with enhanced energy efficiency*. Institute of Science and Technology Policy, Murdoch University, WA. Occasional Discussion Paper 1/93.

British Petroleum (BP) 1994, *Statistical Review of World Energy*, BP, London.

Bulletin 1994, 'Highway Hits a Road Block', 13 September, p. 24.

——— 1995, 'The Bigger Money Will be Spent in WA Waters — Most in the Carnarvon Basin', 14 February, p. 72.

——— 1995a, 'The Gap Begins to Fill', 28 February, p. 80.

Bureau of Resource Sciences (BRS) 1993, *Oil and Gas Resources of Australia 1992*, BRS, Canberra.

——— 1994, *Oil and Gas Resources of Australia 1993*, BRS, Canberra.

Bureau of Transport and Communications Economics (BTCE) 1994, *Economics of Alternative Fuels in Australian Transport*, BTCE, Canberra.

Burtt, E. A. 1932, *The Metaphysical Foundations of Modern Science*, Routledge & Kegan Paul, London, pp. 254–60.

Business in China 1994, 'Car Industry on Highway to Success!' November, p. 15.

Business Review Weekly 1994, Harrison Owen, reported in 'When Losing Control can put you in the Driver's Seat', 21 February, p. 58.

——— 1994a, Dr Michael Gordy, reported in 'The Gap Closes Between Thinking and Doing', 21 March, p. 58.

Campbell, C. 1991, *The Golden Century of Oil 1950–2050*, Kluwer Academic Publishers, Boston.

China Business Review 1994, 'Tantalizing Tarim', July–August, p. 14.

Conn, C. & White, D. 1994, *Revolution in Upstream Oil and Gas*, McKinsey & Co., Sydney.

―――― Costanza, R. 1980, 'Embodied Energy and Economic Valuation', *Science*, no. 210, pp. 1214–19.

―――― 1981, 'Embodied Energy, Energy Analysis, and Economics', in H. E. Daly & A. F. Umana (eds), *Energy, Economics, and the Environment*, Westview, Boulder, Co., pp. 119–46.

Courier-Mail 1994, 'Smog Hits Baby-belt Suburbs', 14 May, p. 4.

―――― 1995, 'Solving the Crawl', 2 May, p. 11.

―――― 1995a, 'Corridor for Buses on Way', 4 July, p. 5.

―――― 1995b, 'Massive Road, Rail Overhaul', 10 July, p. 7.

―――― 1995c, 'Will They Learn?', 1 August, p. 7.

Cox, J. 1994, *Refocussing Road Reform*, Business Council of Australia, Melbourne.

Croxon, H. 1994, 'Transport and the Cost of Living', Fix Australia Fix The Roads Summit (FAFTR), Department of Transport, Perth, 29 April.

Daily Telegraph (London) 1995, 16 February.

Daly, H. 1993, 'The Perils of Free Trade', *Scientific American*, November, p. 24.

Daly, H. & Cobb, J. 1989, *For the Common Good*, Beacon Press, Boston.

Economist 1993, 'A Shocking Speculation About the Price of Oil', 18 September, pp. 69–70.

―――― 1995, 'Saudi Arabia's Future', 18 March, p. 21.

Ecos 1992, 'Getting Drier in the West', Winter issue, p. 6

Fix Australia Fix The Roads Summit (FAFTR) 1994, Discussion Panel, Department of Transport, Perth, 29 April, p. 3.

Gever, J., Kaufmann, R., Skole, D. & Vörösmarty, C. 1991, *Beyond Oil*, University Press of Colorado, Boulder.

Gilchrist, G. 1994, *The Big Switch*, Allen & Unwin, Sydney.

Grace, J. 1995, 'Russian Gas Resource Base: Large, Overstated, Costly to Maintain', *Oil & Gas Journal*, 6 February, p. 71.

Grains Council of Australia 1995, *Milling Wheat Project: Inventing the Future*, Grains Council of Australia, Canberra.

Hall, C., Cleveland, C. & Kaufmann, R. 1986, *Energy and Resource Quality*, Wiley Interscience, New York.

Hills Motorway 1994, *Prospectus*, Hills Motorway Trust, The Hills Motorway Pty Ltd, Sydney.

Hubbert, M. K. 1967, 'Degree of Advancement of Petroleum Exploration in the United States', *The American Association for Petroleum Geologists*, vol. 51, no. 11, pp. 2207–27.

―――― 1969, 'Energy Resources', in National Academy of Sciences National Research Council, *Resources and Man*, W. H. Freeman & Co., San Francisco, pp. 158–242.

IMRA 1991, *Moving Melbourne: A Public Transport Strategy for Inner Melbourne*, Inner Melbourne Regional Association Inc.

Ismail, I. A. H. 1994, 'Capital Limitations, Environmental Movements May Interfere With Expansion Plans', *Oil & Gas Journal*, 9 May, p. 60.

Ivanhoe, L. & Leckie, G. 1993, 'Global Oil, Gas Fields, Sizes Tallied, Analyzed', *Oil & Gas Journal*, 15 February, p. 87.

Kanak, L. & Walker, L. 1989, 'The Reality of World Oil Production, Demand and Future Oil Prices',*Chemical Engineering in Australia*, vol. 14, no. 4, pp. 6–9.

Lewin, R. 1993, *Complexity: Life at the Edge of Chaos*, Dent, London.

Lubulwa, A. 1986, 'ORANI Misinterpretation May Mislead Transport Planners', *Australian Transport*, May, p. 13.

Mair, I. 1995, 'Time for Creative Thinking to Save Water Supplies', *Engineering Times*, Institution of Engineers, Australia, July.

Masters, C. D., Root, D. H. & Attanasi. 1991, 'Resource Constraints in Petroleum Production Potential', *Science*, vol. 253, p. 146.

Maunsell, 1992, *North West Transport Links East Environmental Impact Statement*, Maunsell Pty Ltd & RTA, NSW, p. 33.

Michael, K. 1994, Speech to Fix Australia Fix The Roads Summit (FAFTR), Department of Transport, Perth, 29 April.

Miremadi, A. & Ismail, I. 1993, 'Middle East Due Even Greater Role in World Oil Supply', *Oil & Gas Journal*, 21 June, pp. 61–71

Moon, B. 1994, 'Transport Energy in Australia', *Energy Policy*, vol. 22, no. 4, pp. 331–41.

National Times 1980, 'Rundle Plan Leaves Camm Speechless', 1 March, p. 61.

Newman, P. 1994, *Freeways: A View From the UK*, Institute of Science and Technology Policy, Murdoch University, Perth, 5 July.

Newman, P. & Kenworthy, J. 1991, *Towards a More Sustainable Canberra*, Institute of Science and Technology Policy, Murdoch University, Perth.

Newman, P., Kenworthy, J. & Lyons, T. 1988, 'Does Free Flowing Traffic Save Energy and Lower Traffic Emissions in Cities?', *Search*, vol. 19, nos 5–6, p. 267.

Newman, P. et al. 1994, *Australia's Population Carrying Capacity*, Institute of Science and Technology Policy, Murdoch University, Perth.

New Scientist 1995, 'Report Slam, Official Traffic Forecasts', 7 January, p. 5.

New Ways Not Freeways (NWNF) 1995, Submission on Draft SEQ Integrated Regional Transport Plan, NWNF, Brisbane.

Nicolis, G. 1992, cited in Paul Davies (ed.), *The New Physics*, Cambridge University Press, Cambridge, pp. 325, 344.

Odum, H. 1971, *Environment, Power and Society*, Wiley Interscience, New York.

Odum, H. & Odum, E. 1981, *Energy Basis for Man and Nature*, McGraw-Hill Book Co., New York.

Oil & Gas Australia 1994, 'Dramatic Increase Tipped for Offshore Activity', February, p. 8.

Oil & Gas Journal 1993, 'Russian Petroleum Industry Said to be Struggling for Survival', 13 September, p. 29.

—— 1993a, 'Study Finds FSU Oil Flow Slide Easing', 8 November, pp. 30–3.

—— 1994, 'Need for Refining Capacity Creates Opportunity for Producers in Middle East', 11 July, pp. 37–42.

—— 1994a, 'Industry Pushes for More Access to Offshore Oil and Gas Resources', 18 July, p. 16.

—— 1995, Newsletter, 9 January.

—— 1995a, 'Canadian Firm Foresees Balanced Gas Supply/Demand', 6 February, p. 46.

Oil & Gas Review 1992, 'State Development, Western Australia, Future Developments: Cossack Wanaea', November, pp. 20–1

_____ 1994, 'Western Australian Petroleum Production Forecasts', Department of Resources Development, Western Australia, December, pp. 36–41.

Parramatta Advertiser 1994, 27 July.

Petroleum Economist 1990, 'Soviet Union: How to Stop the Slide', November, pp. 11–12.

_____ 1991, 'UN Attacks Energy Gap', July, p. 17.

_____ 1993, 'Oil Production Plan Prompts Financial Scepticism', February, pp. 3–4.

_____ 1993a, 'Desperately Seeking E & P', February, pp. 11–12.

_____ 1993b, 'Oil Import Deal Heralds Loss of Net Exporter Status', August, p. 35.

_____ 1993c, 'Cash Crisis Looms', September, p. 20.

_____ 1994, 'World Oil Production', February, p. 72.

_____ 1994a, M. Kielman, quoted in 'Saudi Rulers Fail to Measure Up', April, p. 9.

_____ 1995, 'Ministers go on World Tour in an Effort to Get Sanctions Lifted', January, p. 3.

Petroleum Gazette 1990, 'Upward Pressure on World Oil Prices Over Next Ten Years', vol. 25, no. 1, pp. 6–9. AIP, Melbourne. (Abridged version of a paper presented by John Shawley, president of BP Developments Australia Ltd to the ABARE Outlook '90 Conference.)

_____ 1992, 'Low Margins in Oil Jeopardise Satisfaction of Future World Petroleum Demand', vol. 27, no. 1, pp. 16–17 AIP, Melbourne. (Summary of the views of John Browne, managing director of Exploration at British Petroleum, London.)

_____ 1993, 'Innovative Production Engineers Ensure Viable Development of Global Offshore Oil Reserves', vol. 28, no. 3, pp. 12–17, AIP, Melbourne.

_____ 1994, 'Car Ownership a Concern in Control of Urban Congestion', vol. 29, no. 2, pp. 22–26, AIP, Melbourne.

Phipps, Stanley, C. 1993, 'Declining Oil Giants Significant Contributors to US Production', *Oil & Gas Journal*, 4 October, pp. 100–3.

Power, P. 1993, 'Chairman's Address to the 1993 APEA Conference', *APEA Journal*, vol. 33, no. 2.

Prigogine, I. & Stengers, I. 1984, *Order Out of Chaos*, Bantam Books, New York.

Public Transport Users' Association Inc. (PTUA) 1995, *Wrong Way Go Back: The Alternative to Melbourne's Freeway Explosion*, PTUA, Melbourne.

Queensland Government 1995, 'Towards an Integrated Regional Transport Plan for South East Queensland', Discussion paper.

Reed, J., Stocker, L. & Newman, P. 1992, *The Hydrogen Economy: A Western Australian Perspective for the Long Term Future*, Institute of Science and Technology Policy, Murdoch University, Perth.

Saul, J. R. 1992, *Voltaire's Bastards: The Dictatorship of Reason in the West*, Vintage Books, New York.

Science 1995, Editorial, vol. 267, 17 February, p. 943.

Select Committee into Land Conservation 1991, *Final Report*, Legislative Assembly of Western Australia.

Sheehan, P. 1994, 'Beyond Voltaire's Bastards', *Australian Rationalist*, Spring.

Simmons, M. 1995, 'Strong Market Indicators', *World Oil*, February, pp. 23–6.

Soddy, W. 1926, *Wealth, Virtual Wealth and Debt*, Dutton, New York.

Standing Advisory Committee on Trunk Road Assessment (SACTRA) 1994, *Trunk Roads and the Generation of Traffic*, Department of Transport, London.

Stauffer, T. 1994, 'Trends in Oil Production Costs in the Middle East and Elsewhere', *Oil & Gas Journal*, 21 March, pp. 105–7.

Tempest, P. 1993, 'The Changing Structure of the Global Oil and Gas Industry', *APEA Journal*, vol. 33, no. 2.

Toohey, B.O, 1994, *Tumbling Dice*, Heinemann, Melbourne.

Vicroads 1994, *Southern and Western Bypasses: Environmental Impact Statement*, Vicroads, Melbourne, Supplement F, pp. 7, 8, 79, 80.

Walker, R. 1994, 'The Real Toll of the Motorway', *Australian Financial Review*, 29 November, p. 19.

Water Authority of Western Australia (WAWA) 1995, *Perth's Water Future*, WAWA, Perth.

Watt, M. 1982, 'An Energy Analysis of the Australian Food System', PhD thesis, Murdoch University, Perth.

West Australian 1993, 'Oil Industry Sees no Threat to Ningaloo', *Earth 2000*, 17 May, p. 3.

—— 1993a, '$1b Oil, LPG Plan for NW Shelf Cash Flow', 5 October, p. 44.

—— 1994, 'Oil and Gas Overdue to Pay Off', 27 December, p. 59.

—— 1995, 'Team Input Led to Victory', 15 May, p. 74.

—— 1995a, 'Workshops Guide to Farmers in Fight Against Acidity', *Earth 2000*, 7 August, p. 6.

Index